Small Spaces, Beautiful Gardens

Keith Davitt

ROCKPORT

First published in the United States of America by
Rockport Publishers, Inc.
33 Commercial Street
Gloucester, Massachusetts 01930-5089
Telephone: (978) 282-9590
Fax: (978) 283-2742
www.rockpub.com

ISBN 1-56496-973-8

10 9 8 7 6 5 4 3

Cover Design: Stoltze Design
Layout Design: Madison Design and Advertising
Production and Page Layout: Susan Raymond
Garden Plan Illustrations: Mary Lou Nye
Cover Image: Keith Davitt
All Photography by: Keith Davitt

Printed in China

All projects designed and constructed by Keith Davitt.
Project featured on page 98 constructed by Lou Devivo and
Keith Davitt.

Small Spaces, Beautiful Gardens

GLOUCESTER MASSACHUSETTS

ROCKPORT PUBLISHERS

Keith Davitt

Contents

Introduction

We all enjoy a beautiful garden, small or large, and of any kind—an English cottage garden, a Japanese meditation garden, a stone patio surrounded by luxuriant plantings, a water garden, a grassy backyard with shrubs and trees and perennials—any place that is well laid out, carefully and tastefully organized, and developed into a unified environment offering variety, harmony, and pleasurable experiences. And yet, strange to tell, really beautiful gardens are not common in urban and suburban America. On small properties, they are even more rare—though the desire and need for them has never been greater.

Why are really attractive, small gardens so rare? In my view, the reasons are two, and they are simple. Most people don't begin to realize to what extent landscape design is capable of transforming a small property, and if they do think their yard could become a complete delight, they don't know how to bring that about. It isn't that potential gardeners don't care about or want wonderful outdoor living areas. They would love them. But because the apparent limitations of the site seem overwhelming, a wonderful garden appears unachievable to them, and they have no idea how to go about creating one.

The purpose of this book is to address both these issues: to show a variety of pleasing gardens that have been achieved in small spaces and to illuminate principles behind the design of each. Every successful garden succeeds for definite reasons, the principles behind which can be understood and applied. Each of the gardens presented embodies several of these principles at work. For the most part, I photographed these gardens between high bloom times. This is to emphasize their more enduring values—overall design, spatial relationships, form, mass, and texture—rather than the more transient color displays. With the exception of one garden, all were completed within the last several years, so the "bones" of the gardens are easily visible.

Finally, let me add that these are not grand gardens, possible for an elite few only. If we use the number ten to represent an elaborate, expensive landscape—say, in the one hundred thousand dollar range—then most of these gardens would be well under five in terms of complexity and cost and are, especially if built over time, within the reach of the majority of gardeners.

Finding the Design
Consult the Genius of the Place

In designing and building gardens, nothing serves the designer so well as the concept of consulting the genius of the place—opening the higher senses and allowing the place to reveal its quintessential nature, then designing from there. Even the most barren of sites or most artificially derived areas—and no matter how small or uninviting—contains the germane motif or theme around which the garden will be designed. This is one reason why every finished garden, though the space may be the same size and shape as another, is unique.

Upon first encountering a site to design, it is important to take the time to feel the place. Allow the site to generate a reaction, then try to understand just what that reaction is. There may be some things we like: a particular plant overhanging a fence in just such a way, the slope of the ground, a piece of sculpture or the remnants of a stone wall, a piece of lattice or a grouping of plants, a particularly overgrown corner or an open area. These elements convey more than just what they seem to be. A little section of stone wall, for example, may conjure the feeling of an Old World walled garden. A small clearing in the midst of an overgrown area may hint at the charm of a secret garden. A change in elevation may suggest a raised bed or terracing. Somewhere in what is already there resides a theme, a motif from which to build.

Note also the disagreeable elements; there may be many more of these. The place may feel static, tedious, lacking purpose or interest. Wires or buildings may present unpleasant views, or objectionable noises may be all too evident. The garden area may be overgrown or barren. It may be divided into areas too small to invite use or paved in some undesirable material, or it may slope too much. These dislikes are as important as the positive aspects. When a place feels oppressive, static, or dissatisfying in some way, the place itself is saying so. What has been done to the place, or has not been done, despite its potential, set in the context of one's preferences cause the negative reaction. Pay close attention to this sense of dissatisfaction with existing elements, for beginning to eliminate them, even conceptually, also begins the process of unveiling the potential of the place. In the process of identifying and eliminating the negative elements, the site is unburdened of its previously imposed restrictions and moves toward its development as a beautiful, satisfying environment.

If the design motif is elusive, be patient. Very often, the genius of the place does not at first reveal itself, particularly on sites that have been stripped and left flat and empty. Pay close attention to your own quiet notions as they arise, and listen carefully to the comments of family members. A single comment—"I love roses," or "I was wondering about a secret garden"—can illuminate the design approach best suited to the nature of the site. These innocent statements are clues of the utmost importance and should be heeded. The only two ways to improve a site are to reduce the negative and to enhance the positive. Responding to the property in both these departments yields an almost magically reliable starting point in finding a design that is beautiful and enjoyable, and that seems to arise naturally from the site itself.

Enlarging the Garden through Terracing

As the following projects show, elevation changes, or terraces, are an important consideration in the creation of small gardens. Many small spaces can be made to feel larger by appropriate terracing. Some benefit from reducing the number of terraces; others respond to the added interest and dimension of new terracing. The reasons have to do with how well the different spaces created by terracing accommodate visitors to the garden, how comfortable they make them feel. Naturally, sloped sites often lend themselves to terracing and are generally more accommodating and look larger when terraced, but that effect can be achieved in many ways.

Too many planes, or one that is too large, can be as uninviting as too few or one that is too small. Watch out for an elevation level that is too cramped for its intended use—it can also be discomforting. When the proportions between the height of a raised terrace and the flat area before or behind it are off, the whole fails.

Bear in mind that the materials used to create the terraces have an important impact on the overall feel of the garden, as does the line the retaining walls are given. In some designs, straight lines and geometrically shaped spaces are appropriate; in others, curves or a more free-form style is best. As is true of all elements of a design, these decisions should arise from the theme or motif of the garden as an integrated, unified space.

This chapter presents several gardens in which terracing is paramount to the design and demonstrates how it is handled differently in each one.

Whimsical Family Garden

Taming a Small Garden

Complexity Level 4

Garden size:
19 feet wide × 22 feet deep
(5.8 meters wide × 6.7 meters deep)

Even though this small yard violated nearly every principle of gracious design, it had a definite aura of charm. A few plants took up a lot of space, and many neighboring plants encroached on the yard. Linear and cluttered, the space was divided into three unusable planes, making the area seem much smaller than it really was. Yet within all this good-natured mayhem, there was something delightfully appealing: a delicate birch in the yard; a young and handsome larch next door; an unruly wisteria on the wires above; a graceful kerria dangling its blossoming branches over the fence; and everywhere a luxuriance of neighborly plantings crossing the boundaries. This childlike, unruly charm was key and, in conjunction with the Victorian theme of the home, would be the motif that guided the development of the design.

Above: Before redesign, poor division of space made this small garden space seem even smaller.

A tiny, unusable space was made into a family's outdoor living room.

Small Garden
—•—
Wisdom

**Three key design techniques helped
to make this small garden seem larger:**

- ❀ Divide space to create a sense of expansiveness.
- ❀ Use detail (walls, lattice, benches, fountain, tiles)
  to add dimension.
- ❀ Maintain proper proportion between planting beds
  and patio or paving.

To Make Space, Remove Unwanted Elements

Start your small garden redesign by removing undesirable elements, even if only on paper. Divest your garden of unwanted plants, walls, and surfaces, and a clearer picture will begin to form about what you do want to see there. In this project, the original theme of a sort of vivacious charm needed to be freed of restricting elements before it could be developed.

Once the site was cleared on paper, all of the everyday uses for the garden—entertaining, cooking, dining, and, for the children, playing—needed to be addressed. The space measured only 19 feet wide by 22 feet deep (5.8 meters wide by 6.7 meters deep), yet, as is often the case, more space was available here than was at first apparent.

Top: The same view as above, after the walls were completed.

Above: Once the clutter was removed from the site, the walls were chalked out and staked.

Organize Small Gardens Wisely

How you divide and organize a small garden has the utmost effect on the perception of spaciousness. Here, three separate elevations had been created by the railroad tie and log divisions. We perceive space by how we are physically accommodated by it, determined by the boundaries imposed; this garden had too many boundaries creating spaces into which we were not at all well accommodated. Even though the elevation changes were small, they added to the problem: The result was discomfort and a sense of confinement.

Because the garden was too small for more than two distinct areas, a single living area bordered on three sides with raised beds works well. Raised areas permit abundant planting not subject to the vigor of children's feet, and the larger, paved area provides ample outdoor living space. The initial design also includes a playhouse, symmetrical brick bed walls, and a central water garden. Random rectangular bluestone with river-stone joints to lighten the look made an attractive, serviceable paving. Did other possibilities exist, perhaps more relaxed and less symmetrical? In every small garden, there is usually more than one solution to every problem.

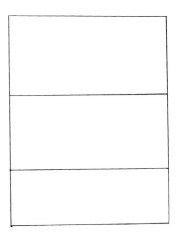

A space divided into three small areas feels restrictive.

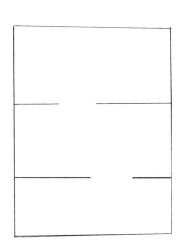

To increase the visual expanse of each area and, thus, of the entire space, access points between areas are emphasized.

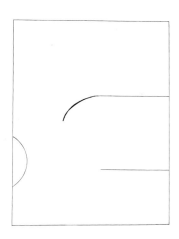

The three small areas are further integrated to make the space seem larger still.

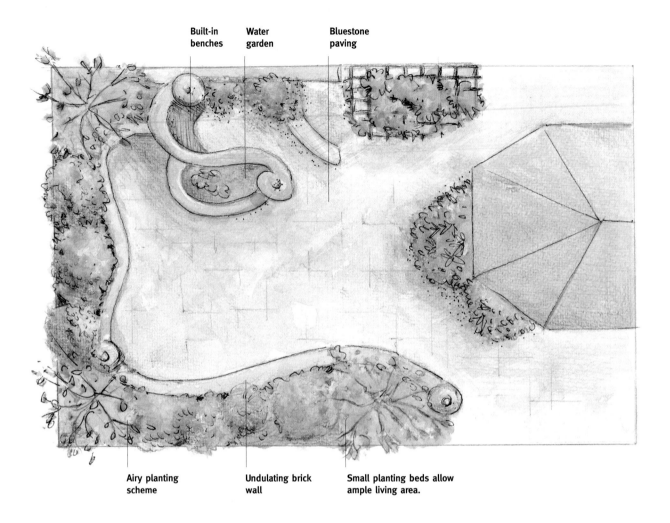

Built-in benches   **Water garden**   **Bluestone paving**

Airy planting scheme   **Undulating brick wall**   **Small planting beds allow ample living area.**

Exploring the Design of a Small Garden

Above: Final design plan. Note that the playhouse was eliminated, and the wall is shown in more than one possible layout.

Designing a garden of any size is a process of discovery and unfolding rather than a single act. The first drawings are exploratory and not always meant to provide the precise design approach that will become the garden.

In the process of designing a garden, whether or not you use a landscape designer, you need to build around a theme or concept, keeping what you like and discarding what does not make you happy, until, finally, a completed design emerges in which every component contributes to the whole.

Formality versus Femininity

Although the final plan contains all the elements of the original plan—the low brick walls, the patio, water garden, and playhouse—it has none of the formality of the first. The final plan omits the symmetry and geometry without sacrificing the balance. Symmetry almost always conveys formality, as do geometric lines. Such strongly architectural layouts are perceived as more masculine and tend to feel rigid. Curvy lines are feminine, softer, and can convey a feeling of cheerfulness or even jubilation. The sense of structure is less, so a feeling of freedom and lightness can come across.

In the final free-form design motif, winding curved walls replace the more formal walls and delineate the beds. To remain true to the Victorian-style house, the walls and coping are both brick. The water garden is placed centrally along the long axis as a major focal point.

Don't Be Afraid of Change

Experience teaches that even when a working plan is in hand, with every detail agreed upon and construction begun, changes may follow. Design plans, however excellent, are drawn in pencil on paper—they are not carved in stone. In actuality, it is rare for a garden to be built precisely according to plan, as new ideas, forgotten wish-list items, and site features often require modifying the final plan.

Consider such changes opportunities to improve a design, not merely to change it and certainly not to compromise it. This project changed along the way to completion: a seating bench was installed along the wall, the playhouse was replaced by an arbor, and the site itself demanded a slightly different wall layout because of major birch-tree roots. The free-form design made this easy to accommodate. The other alterations were responses to the design itself. To underscore the playful aspect of the garden, the serpentine walls rise and fall in an undulant motion. Hand-carved tiles of animals and family members' names are randomly built into the wall to enhance the whimsical quality of the garden.

Good Fences Make Good Gardens

FENCES NOT ONLY SEPARATE ONE PROPERTY FROM ANOTHER, THEY PROVIDE THE OUTER STRUCTURE OF THE GARDEN AND AFFECT THE OVERALL LOOK AND FEEL OF THE SPACE. IN THIS PROJECT, A LIGHT AND SIMPLE LATTICE CREATING ONLY A PARTIAL SEPARATION FROM THE NEIGHBORING GARDENS WAS CHOSEN TO MAINTAIN A FREE AND EASY FEEL.

Why This Small Garden Works

Here are four key design techniques employed in this urban garden project that you can use singly or together to visually expand your small garden.

First, and most important, aim for a small garden design that has unity, with each of the components contributing to the overall effect. This garden design is strong and durable, yet light, airy, charming, and whimsical. A two-course thick brick wall can be a serious element but here, as it winds in and out and rolls up and down, filled with animals in relief and built-in benches, it is something else altogether. The wavy walls, water garden, winding stairs, and arching arbor work together to produce an environment that is functional, yet fun and graceful. Even the paving is light and reminiscent of river flats and river pebbles.

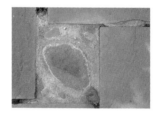

Above: River stones break up the symmetry of flagstone paving, adding a touch of lightness.

Right Top: A wavy wall of brick with hand-carved tiles creates a raised planting bed.

Right Bottom: A water garden with a frog spout brings a playful element into the garden.

Proportion Makes All the Difference

Small spaces are especially sensitive to spatial imbalance, so it is important to pay attention to proper proportion in their design. Play with the relative sizes of the hardscape elements (patios, walls, walkways) and the softscape elements (planting beds) of your garden until they feel right. In this project, narrower beds would have provided more room in the patio but constricted the planting areas. Overly large planting areas would have sacrificed living area. As it is, the beds are no larger than necessary to accommodate ample planting. These are the proportions that succeeded, both functionally and visually: a two-to-one ratio of patio to planting on any one side of the garden, with an overall equal ratio of planting to paving.

Top: The two-to-one ratio of patio to plantings on each side of the garden yields a small garden that is functional as well as beautiful.

Above: Apparently remote or separated areas within even very small gardens contribute to a sense of spaciousness.

Create Spaces Within Space

Carve out separate spaces from the main area to create the illusion of more space. The private seating area built into the wall behind the water garden and the curve outs in the two upper corners make the main living area seem much roomier by contrast. At the same time, these seating areas have an almost arbitrary aspect that contributes to the overall whimsical design theme.

Detail Adds Dimension

Adding detail to a small garden creates a visual impression of roominess. What, after all, happens when you enter a garden? You respond, perhaps unknowingly, to its influence upon you. If there are visual attractions, fragrances, sounds to experience, you become involved in the garden. When you leave, you don't remember it as a three-dimensional area but as an experiential environment that affected you in many ways. That sense of expansion through detail is exactly what happens in this garden. The animal tiles, the water garden with its exotic plants and wildlife and spewing stream, the shells and beads worked into the masonry, are details that attract and contribute to one's enjoyment of the garden.

The planting also contributes to the garden's overall theme and was designed to provide a range of sensory experiences through the seasons. Bearing blueberry plants offer fruit for breakfast and emit a pleasant fragrance when brushed. Grasses remain attractive through the winter, as do the berry-bearing skimmia, the holly, and the oak-leaf hydrangea. Honeysuckle perfumes the air and, with clematis and rose, covers the lattice. Flowering shrubs and perennials brighten the garden from early spring to early winter. In all, the planting is light, leafy, seemingly arbitrary, yet unified through repetition of species, textural qualities, and foliage color.

Above: Use details to create a visual impression of roominess. These hand-carved tiles of animals and the names of family members add another dimension of enjoyment to the wall and the garden.

Design theme
Before: Derived from the carefree, unruly vivacity of the site. *(top left)*

Organization of space
After: Three areas were combined into one large space with a raised planting area retained by a curvy brick wall. Two almost independent, smaller areas become one large space. *(top right)*

Structure
Raised planter walls and brick water garden add structure but are lightened by their line and by built-in animal tiles. A raised fountain, two built-in benches, and an arbor also add strength and structure. *(middle left)*

Lessons from a Small Garden

Boundary structure
A perimeter fence made of a simple lattice without a cap maintains a light and informal feeling; the perforated fencing will fade into the planting. *(middle right)*

Combination of materials
Brick walls and bluestone paving. River stones set into the paving lighten the look and keep the design informal. *(bottom left)*

Proportion
Planting beds are small to enough allow ample living area. Low retaining walls do not dominate the living areas. *(bottom right)*

Summary of Details
Tiles and shells in the masonry, curvy walls, water garden, river stone, light lattice, small spaces, built-in benches, frog fountain, airy planting scheme with points of structure.

Garden in Three Parts

I: English Terraced Garden
Adding Structure and Movement to the Small Garden

Complexity Level 3

Garden size:
35 feet wide × 35 feet deep
(10.7 meters wide x 10.7 meters deep)

The natural layout of a garden may indicate distinct areas that each require individual treatment and the application of different principles. Though the three independent areas in this garden needed a unifying theme, their relationship did not need to be obvious. Each area would have its own unique character but would also exist in harmony with each of the other areas, with the first transitioning comfortably into the second and the second into the third. We will look at these three areas in turn, beginning with the street-side garden.

Above: The before image shows a sloping yard devoid of beauty or interest.

ROSE GATE

The English garden is characterized by an abundance of flora.

Three design techniques generate interest and movement on a static, bland slope:

❀ Visually enlarge a sloping garden with terracing.
❀ Make sure the flat areas formed by the terracing are of useful size.
❀ Generate a sense of movement with curved retaining walls and winding paths.

Area III

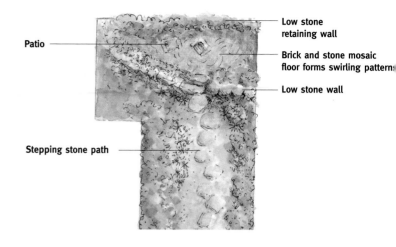

Patio

Low stone
retaining wall

Brick and stone mosaic
floor forms swirling patterns

Low stone wall

Stepping stone path

Area II

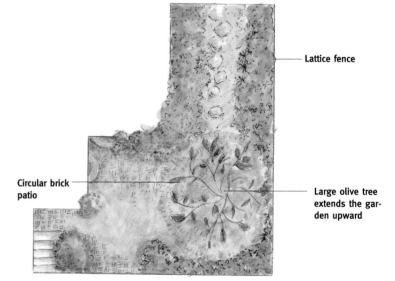

Lattice fence

Circular brick
patio

Large olive tree
extends the gar-
den upward

Area I

Arbor

Winding
brick walkway

Occasional
stone in
walkway

Curving stone
walls

Terracing the slopes adds
dimension and enlarges
the small garden.

*A view of the garden
plan in three parts.
See page 30 for
details on area two
and page 33 for
area three.*

Overcome Discouraging Slopes and Tedious Straight Lines

Curving walls and walkway and an abundance of plantings transform this once static, stagnant yard into an English terraced garden flowing with motion and beauty. The before images reveal a disquieting garden space featuring a straight brick walk that cut through a drab expanse of sloping lawn between the road and the house. Not only was the site not pretty, it was offensive. Nothing had been done to bring grace or charm or magic or interest to the place. Even a better lawn and a few plants would not have been adequate. The want of steps accentuated the bleakness of the situation, and the yard's completely open aspect caused the whole scene to be instantly apprehended by the eye. The result was rigid, unappealing, and depressing.

However, the people who bought this property for their retirement home dreamed of building an English garden there. The details of the dream, however, were not specified. An English garden, after all, can be many things, from sprawling perennial beds to a distinctly formal layout with hedges and topiary.

Blend Nature with Architecture

STONE IS A WONDERFUL ELEMENT TO INCORPORATE IN A GARDEN, WHETHER AS WALLS, IN A ROCK OR WATER GARDEN, OR PLACED STRATEGICALLY ABOUT. IT BLENDS NATURE WITH ARCHITECTURE, ADORNING THE TERRAIN WHILE COMBINING BEAUTIFULLY WITH PLANTS, SHOWING BOTH FOLIAGE AND FLOWERS TO GREAT ADVANTAGE. IT WEATHERS WELL, GROWS MORE ATTRACTIVE WITH AGE, AND, WHEN LAID DRY, BECOMES HOME TO VOLUNTEER PLANTS, THUS APPEARING SOFTER AND MORE ORGANIC.

Personal taste, site analysis, and an appreciation of the beautiful seaside locale soon eliminated the formal layout option and gradually revealed the design waiting to be realized. Within sound of the ocean, open and sunny on clear days, shrouded in fog on others, the land sloping slightly from the house to the road—this place was made to become a terraced garden. The notion of an English garden suggested a plethora of beautiful plants in magnificent disorder spilling over the tops of stone, from within the cracks and creeping up the base of the walls.

Right: The strength created by terracing with stone permits an abundance of planting without generating a sense of confusion.

Terracing the slope expanded the space into three ample planes.

Build Dimension and Interest with Terracing

Terracing can visually enlarge a space. Whereas the last garden before redesigning was broken into three areas and seemed restrictive and uninviting before leveling, this yard was one plane sloping from the house area down to the road, and it looked small. After terracing, it appears much larger and considerably more interesting. So why did one garden benefit by having the terraces removed and another benefit by adding them?

Compare the image of the property after the walls were built to the original view. As the photo of the property just after the walls were built shows, the site looks enormous in comparison to what it seemed before terracing. A slope almost invariably makes a site look smaller than it actually is. Take any grade and level it, and the available area will seem to have increased.

Had one wall been placed near the road and the site leveled behind it, the site would have instantly seemed much larger than before, but less so than it does now. The large plane thus created behind the wall would have been foreshortened in our sight and appear smaller than its actual dimensions. Building two walls, thereby creating three levels, each amply large enough to invite use, made the site seem much roomier than before terracing. In addition, the elevation changes add dimension and the walls add interest—again, contributing to a sense of expansion.

Create Pleasing Proportions

When building retaining walls, remember that the total height of the walls equals the difference in grade elevation from the lowest to the highest points if the terrain between is level. In this instance, there was a 5 1/2-foot (1.7 m) elevation drop from the highest point to the lowest. Had a single wall been used, it would have needed to be 5 1/2 feet (1.7 m) tall—so dominating the areas before and behind it as to absolutely destroy any sense of spaciousness. Three walls would have chopped the yard into uninviting areas and failed thereby. Two walls, each about 30 inches (76 cm) tall, were just what was needed to maximize the usable areas and create pleasing proportions between the vertical and horizontal planes.

Use Curves to Soften Straight Lines

CURVES CAN DO MUCH TO SOFTEN, RELAX, AND EXPAND THE STRAIGHT LINES AND HARD SURFACES USUALLY ENCOUNTERED IN GARDENS. THEY PROVIDE A LYRICAL SENSE OF MOTION, HELPING ALLEVIATE THE RIGIDITY THAT ACCOMPANIES THE UNAVOIDABLE STRAIGHT LINES OF BUILDINGS AND SUCH. INCORPORATE GRACEFUL CURVES INTO WALLS, WALKWAYS, PLANTING BEDS, PATIOS, GARDEN FURNITURE, WATER GARDENS, AND NEARLY ANY OTHER COMPONENT OF YOUR GARDEN.

These walls arch inward, generating a sense of motion enhanced in the upper wall with the reverse curve on the left. The lower wall also arches inward, but here, the line of the walkway at the driveway end picks up the line of the wall, leading the eye in a long and graceful sweep across the entire expanse. This sweep is experienced as motion. The walls are built of a local sedimentary stone much like that found in England, and laid dry, in keeping with tradition. Tight joints and level courses give it a satisfying, well-built look. Being mortarless and possessed of niches, plants can grow within it, softening and enlivening the construction.

Right: The harmonizing curves of walls and walk generate a sense of flowing motion.

Far right: A mortarless wall provides a home for plants.

The Most Pleasant Distance Between Two Points

In keeping with the overall layout, the straight walk was replaced with a curving brick walkway that winds through the garden, carrying the graceful strength of the walls throughout the expanse. Although a straight line is a more efficient way to travel, a curve is more satisfying. It lets you know that you are in a garden. It slows you down and nearly insists you look around and enjoy what has been laid out for your viewing pleasure. Laid on sand, with the outer courses set in cement, this walk maintains a soft, natural look without sacrificing durability. As brick was randomly worked into the walls, so too was stone incorporated into the walkway, uniting these two structural components with a casual element often found in English country homes and gardens.

Note the integration of the wall with the walkway—the flow of the lines and the physical binding of one to the other. To help blend the walls into the walkway, slightly rounded stones were selected, then their outside edge chiseled to enhance the curve. This binding of walk to wall helps convey a sense of unity and integrity that, if not consciously comprehended, is at least viscerally felt.

The walls bring a satisfying structure to the garden and, together with the winding walkway, unify it so thoroughly that an eclectic bounty of planting was possible without generating the usual hodgepodge effect. A garden with less architectural impact could not sustain such sprawling abundance. Through this floral luxuriance, the visitor is led to the entrance of the second area, the patio and courtyard garden.

Left: A meandering brick walk winds through the garden, uniting the three terraces.

Right: Walk and wall were integrated through careful construction and by incorporating materials from each in the other.

Lessons from a Small Garden

Design theme
English garden, equal parts owners' dream, the sloping nature of the property, and the microclimate. *(top left)*

Organization of space
Two dry-laid stone walls create three planes united by a winding brick walk. *(top right)*

Structure
The walls and the brick walk provide sufficient structure to permit an abundance of planting. *(middle left)*

Boundary structure
Only plants define the side boundaries. *(middle right)*

Combination of materials
Brick and terra-cotta drain-tile insets ornament stone walls, and stone insets lend an informal aspect to the brick walk. *(bottom left)*

Proportion
The walls are as high as possible without dominating the horizontal spaces before and behind. Generally, they are about one third as high as the planes they create. *(bottom right)*

Summary of Details
Curving walls and walk add flow and motion, while the intermixture of materials adds interest.

II: Courtyard Garden

Uniting Areas within the Garden

Complexity Level 3

Garden size:
15 feet wide × 18 feet deep
(4.6 meters wide × 5.6 meters deep)

This courtyard garden serves as another terrace to the front garden, joined to it by the rose arbor. Here, one enters the main outdoor living area, adjacent to the main entrance to the house and to the dining room. An ancient olive tree dominates the space and is the focal point around which the garden was developed. In fact, the existence of this tree determined the design of the courtyard garden. Removing it was unthinkable, and ignoring it both impossible and undesirable.

Above: A courtyard garden.

Small Garden ● Wisdom

Use these ideas to expand a small garden while generating a sense of unity and a feeling of warmth:

❋ Emphasize the garden's vertical dimension with trees.
❋ Enclose outdoor living spaces with plantings.
❋ Reinforce unity by repeating distinctive shapes throughout the garden.

Use the Vertical Dimension

Upward space is as important as the ground level, and in a small garden offers another dimension of possibilities. Include trees, bird houses, and sculpture to extend the compass of the garden. In addition to being a focal point, this olive tree creates a vertical dimension and permits hanging baskets, wind chimes, and such to expand the garden upward. This is often one of the most desirable reasons for including trees in the landscape and why gardens without elements rising above the general planting plane can seem and, in fact, be two-dimensional.

Achieve Unity Through Repetition

To unite one section of a garden with another, repeat the use of primary building materials and distinctive forms. Here, in harmony with the brick walkway leading through the terraced garden, used brick was chosen as the patio material for the second. Likewise in keeping with the motif of the terraced area, stone was worked randomly into the patio. These repetitions of materials relate the front walled garden to the patio garden.

Further, the brick walk extends to the two entry doors, before which are little steps. These curved entry steps, built of brick and stone, were designed to reflect, in much reduced scale, the walls of the front garden. Though the connection is not apparent to most people, it is subliminally felt, and the sense of unity is conveyed through deeper levels of consciousness. This is a subtlety, certainly, but not an unimportant one.

The circular patio was allowed to merge with the walkway leading through the arbor in a natural line, creating attractive planting beds to both right and left. These beds enclose the patio and partially separate it from the house, giving a sense of containment and privacy while seated or dining outdoors.

Left: In the courtyard garden, respect for the venerable olive tree, which had stood for at least fifty years, led to a design layout featuring a semicircular patio with the tree at the center.

This is the sort of patio garden that lends itself to personalization. (As would not be appropriate, for example, in a formal, rectilinear, or very structured patio garden.) Randomly placed pots, favorite planters, small sculptures, and decorative items dropped randomly about all help create a sense of place individualized to the owners. This extension of the warmth and casual friendliness inherent in the design is precisely what makes the spot so agreeable. Being so, it draws its owners from the enclosure of their home into their garden, where they spend many a sunny afternoon and lovely evening—certainly one of the finest and simplest uses of a garden.

Separate Outdoor Living Areas from Buildings

GENERALLY, YOU DO NOT WANT TO FEEL AS IF YOU ARE IN AN EXTENSION OF A BUILDING WHEN YOU ARE IN A GARDEN; YOU WANT TO EXPERIENCE THE GARDEN ITSELF. PLANTS, MORE THAN ANY OTHER ELEMENT, HELP ACHIEVE THIS. IF THE PLANTED AREAS AGAINST THE HOUSE ADORN AND SOFTEN THE ARCHITECTURE, YOU CAN KEEP THE BED PLANTINGS THAT ENCLOSE THE PATIO LOW. IF YOUR HOME IS OF A HARSHER ARCHITECTURE, OR PLANTING SPACES HAVE NOT BEEN CREATED AGAINST THE HOUSE, CHOOSE TALL, FULL PLANTS FOR THE ENCLOSING BEDS TO HELP ACHIEVE SEPARATION.

Lessons from a Small Garden

Design theme
The old olive tree had such presence that the garden design was developed around it.

Organization of space
The round patio area is slightly separated from the house by planting beds.

Structure
The olive tree, the house itself, and the patio are the structural elements of this garden space.

Boundary structure
The lattice fence lends a warmly elegant element to the otherwise informal but well-defined garden room.

Combination of materials
As in the front garden, stone and brick, with foliage and flowers, are the primary elements; chosen to harmonize with the wood of the home.

Proportion
The walkway and patio are just large enough to accommodate easy use. The ratio of paving to planting is about two to one, which, given the softness and warmth of the brick and stone, works.

Summary of Details
The low steps add a delicate element. Their brick and stone construction unites with both the front garden and the patio. That every third course of the patio is made of half-bricks keeps it from being too static. Hanging baskets in the tree carry the garden upward, and the lattice fence gives a finished, elegantly enclosed feeling to the garden.

III: Morning Seating Area
Adorning the Garden with Mosaic

**Complexity
Level 4**

Garden size:
12 feet wide × 6 feet deep
(3.7 meters wide × 1.9 meters deep)

A simple path of stone groupings set in the ground and surrounded by lush plantings leads the way to the section of the garden in the rear of the property. This transitional swath of verdure and flowers makes a pleasant contrast to the hardscape elements. Intended simply as a pass-through garden area, it provides a refreshing break from structural elements and sets off the two structural areas it joins.

Above: A simple path of stone, flanked by its own plant groupings, leads from the courtyard garden to the morning seating area.

Small Garden — Wisdom

Try these approaches to defining smaller areas of the garden:

❀ Articulate transitional areas to distinguish the garden rooms they join.
❀ Use standout decorative elements to anchor small gardens.
❀ Repeat, in reduced size, structural elements found in main areas of the garden.

Express Garden Transitions Clearly

EVEN SMALL GARDENS MAY CONTAIN TRANSITIONAL AREAS, IF ONLY A FEW FEET IN LENGTH. IN SMALL GARDENS, ESPECIALLY, THESE AREAS SHOULD NOT BE BLURRED INTO A KIND OF "NO-MAN'S LAND" BUT SHOULD BE GIVEN DEFINITION IN ORDER TO ACCENTUATE THE VARIETY THE GARDEN OFFERS. ARBORS, FOR EXAMPLE, CAN CONTRIBUTE TO A SENSE OF EXPANSIVE-NESS. THESE TRANSITIONAL POINTS BOTH UNITE AND SEPARATE TWO DISTINCT GARDEN ROOMS, AND PAS-SAGE THROUGH THEM INSTILLS A PALPABLE SENSE OF LEAVING ONE PLACE AND ENTERING ANOTHER.

Above: A morning seating area comprises two thousand pieces of hand-shaped brick and stone laid in a distinctive pattern, reminiscent of water flowing or the branching of leaves.

Opposite: The use of brick and stone and the low retaining walls reflect the front and mid-dle gardens, uniting with them and creating a sense of place.

The concept of unity through repetition reaches its climax in the third garden, whose focal point is a mosaic comprising two thousand pieces of hand-chipped brick and stone laid in swirling patterns that flow into one another. This unusual element makes the spot particularly distinc-tive—a macrocosm of the entire landscape—as well as a place to enjoy the morning sun. The sense of flow and motion through brick and stone, developed in the previous two areas of the garden, is highlighted here in the mosaic. One can spend many a pleasant moment tracing the fluid streams of chipped brick and stone as they swirl and eddy at one's feet. This hand-built mosaic concentrates energy in the morning seating garden and assures a permanent place in one's memory, thereby expanding the garden beyond its spatial dimensions.

Smaller versions of the walls found in the front garden retain the mosaic and wind through this portion of the property, creating planting beds and bringing the front to the back. The three gar-dens—the mosaic, the patio, and the walled garden—express both their independence and their unity. Each area has its own character and charm, but even though they offer tremendous vari-ety, together they convey a sense of wholeness, and thus of completeness, that is satisfying to experience.

Include Ornament in the Garden

DON'T IGNORE THE IMPOR-
TANCE OF ORNAMENT IN THE
GARDEN. PLANTS ALONE
MAY A GARDEN MAKE, BUT
THEY DO NOT MAKE A
LANDSCAPE. STRUCTURES,
ELEVATIONS, WATER FEA-
TURES, TILES—DECORATIVE
ELEMENTS OF ALL SORTS
VERY MUCH BELONG IN THE
GARDEN, EXACTLY AS PAINT-
INGS BELONG ON WALLS
AND CARPETS ON FLOORS.

Lessons from a Small Garden

Design theme
A distinctive mosaic embellishes and adorns a practical seating area in a remote corner of the property.

Organization of space
The third garden is reached through a transitional planting walk that offsets the two structure-defined gardens it connects. The seating area is a self-contained island bounded by structure and surrounded by planting.

Structure
The handmade mosaic seating area, the low wall behind it, and the slightly taller wall in front provide ample structure.

Boundary structure
The natural wood fence with vines creates privacy without the feeling of confinement.

Combination of materials
Brick, stone, and wood nearly always work well together, especially in the company of foliage and flowers.

Proportion
Very low walls are in keeping with the small seating area, which is designed to comfortably accommodate two or three people.

Summary of Details
The mosaic is richly detailed, with three streams or branches of stone and brick flowing into one another, creating eddies or rosettes.

Terraced Delight in Suburbia

Enlivening a Small Front Yard

**Complexity
Level 2**

Garden size:
20 feet wide × 18 feet deep
(6.1 meters wide × 5.5 meters deep)

Sometimes the purpose of terracing is not to enlarge a garden in a linear way but to add dimensionality and interest. Consider this little suburban landscape before redesigning— lawn, foundation plants, annuals, and an overpowering Spruce. Even an abundance of foundation plantings could not have saved this yard from the depressing paradigm to which it belonged, along with millions of others like it across America. Fortunately, the owner too found this front yard garden insipid and wanted to express something more suited to her own temperament and taste, something wild, lush, abundant, and rich— but not too expensive. A worthy challenge indeed.

The Spruce loomed large as a question demanding an answer. A mature tree should not be eliminated without serious thought, but this one was awkward and out of place. In truth, such a tree should never have been planted so close to a house and in so small a yard. It overpowered the space, rubbed against the building, and cast shade on the primary garden areas. After careful consideration, the decision was made to remove the tree.

Above: This static, dreary, and unimaginative suburban front yard was hiding the exuberance that lay in wait.

An abundance of foliage rising through three elevations creates vertical dimensionality across a horizontal sweep of plantings.

Small Garden
Wisdom

Things to consider when redesigning a front yard:

* ❀ Weigh the pros and cons before removing any mature trees.
* ❀ Free yourself of the idea that streetside yards are for the neighbors, not you.
* ❀ Create drama with the use of harmonies and contrasts in planting.

Terraces Need Not Be Flat

Avoid Creating Secondary Problems

BE CAREFUL NOT TO SOLVE ONE PROBLEM ONLY TO CREATE ANOTHER. THE CONCRETE FOUNDATION COULD HAVE BEEN EASILY MASKED BY BUILDING ONLY ONE WALL, BACKFILLING, AND PLANTING, BUT A TROUBLESOME ELEMENT WOULD HAVE BEEN CREATED— A TALL WALL FAIRLY CLOSE TO THE STREET. NOT ONLY WOULD THIS HAVE INVITED SMALL CHILDREN TO PLAY (WHICH THEY DO FREELY IN THIS ROCKWELLIAN FAMILY NEIGHBORHOOD), POSSIBLY LEADING TO FALLS, IT WOULD HAVE LOOKED ALTOGETHER TOO IMPOSING. THE TWO TERRACING WALLS SOLUTION AVOIDED THESE SECONDARY PROBLEMS AND ALLOWED A GENTLE TRANSITION FROM STREET TO FOUNDATION.

Right: Design plan for a suburban front yard garden.

This opened the space and revealed all its sad unloveliness. The concrete foundation leapt brutally into view and called out for cover. As it supports the porch, it had to stay, but that raised foundation suggested the notion of terracing. The owner's expressed appreciation for color and abundance and her distaste for the static yard also led to this design approach. The thought was that terraces would add vitality and dimensionality, and arching them would inject an element of gracefulness, so wanting in this space. The areas created by terracing would provide abundant planting areas—and abundance, it seemed, should be a guiding force behind all that followed.

One wall would have been sufficient, but the notion of a water garden was appealing. In order to place it near the house, where it would pose no problem within the neighborhood and could be enjoyed from the glassed-in living room, a wall nearly as tall as the existing foundation would be necessary to retain it. That seemed too tall a structure to impose on the yard, especially as it would be closer to the sidewalk than the foundation wall. Two walls forming three elevations solved the problem. The upper wall now supports the water garden, which comes right up to the edge of the porch, and the lower wall allows a gradual, graceful step to ground level. Curving the walls provided that element of motion and softness so lacking here.

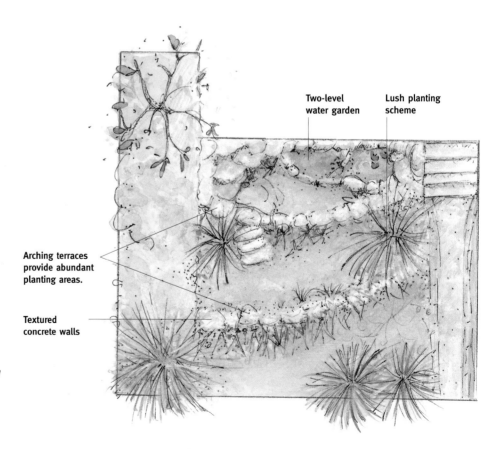

Two-level water garden

Lush planting scheme

Arching terraces provide abundant planting areas.

Textured concrete walls

Manufactured retaining blocks harmonize better with this neighborhood than would natural stone.

Working within a Budget

If time and money are limited, it is often possible and sometimes necessary to find alternative materials. In this instance, textured concrete blocks were chosen over fieldstone to build the terraced walls. Prefabricated concrete interlocking blocks designed for this purpose are not less expensive than stone but infinitely easier, and therefore quicker, to work with. Once the bottom footing trench is cut and leveled and the first course set, it is simply a matter of stacking the blocks. In this case, the blocks seem a better choice than fieldstone even from a purely aesthetic viewpoint. Fieldstone would have looked good in itself but would probably have contrasted too much with the overall environment. The textured concrete blocks retain the soil as well as stone but harmonize better with the house and the surrounding materials of the neighborhood.

In Suburbia, Design in Harmony with the Neighborhood

FRONT YARDS, UNLIKE REAR PROPERTIES, ARE NOT ISOLATED, STAND-ALONE SPACES. RATHER, THEY ARE USUALLY A PART OF THE LARGER WHOLE OF THE NEIGHBORHOOD, WITH WHICH THEIR DESIGN SHOULD HARMONIZE. THIS DOES NOT MEAN THE YARD NEED CONFORM TO THE USUAL SUBURBAN SCHEME—IT CAN, AND PERHAPS SHOULD BE, VERY DIFFERENT. BUT THE MATERIALS USED SHOULD NOT OVERTLY CLASH WITH THE OTHER BUILDING MATERIALS SEEN IN THE SAME VIEW, AND THE GARDEN SHOULD POSE NO AESTHETIC THREAT TO NEIGHBORING PROPERTIES.

A two-part water garden with waterfall, fish, and aquatic flora.

Design Your Garden for Your Own Enjoyment

A sweep of lawn unites this garden with the neighborhood while contributing to the gracefulness of its own landscape.

As you design your garden, be sure to study and include what makes you happy about a garden. Front yards are sometimes designed with sidewalk appeal—a benighted notion from the 1950s. The idea was to increase property value by making it look good from the street and sidewalk, never mind the enjoyment of the owners. Here, that notion was cast aside, and though the property looks wonderful from the sidewalk, it was designed with the owner's pleasure in mind. The water garden, for example, can be seen only from the porch and living room. With a waterfall into the upper pool, which flows into the second and provides sound and motion, with the koi, frog, and water plants, the water garden brings enormous enjoyment to the owner through most of the year.

In part because it is a pleasant medium in itself, both to see and to walk on, and in part to maintain continuity with the neighboring properties, a portion of lawn was retained. Giving it a flowing shape rather than the usual static rectangle added interest and offset the planting and retaining walls as well.

Fill Terraces with Foliage and Flowers

The two tiers, backfilled with topsoil, provide wonderful planting beds for a plethora of foliage and flowers. Choose plants from the great variety available at wholesale nurseries, and select your favorites under the guidance of professional experience. This owner did just that, and the result was exactly what she wished. From spring through fall, something is always blooming, and at peak times the garden is spectacular.

In addition, the two curving walls, the two-level water garden, and the luxuriant plantings add a refreshing dimensionality normally lacking in the suburban landscape. Not only do the plantings sweep into the lawn, carving out gracefully curving beds, but they also go up. The eye is swept along horizontally and then elevated through stages of richly endowed planting planes.

A plethora of species yields rich textural and form contrasts and harmonies.

Harmonies and Contrasts

The mass effect here is important. It is a bold, unequivocal statement and a sincere expression of the owner. But the details too are significant, views of which change as one moves through the garden. Note particularly the use of harmonies and contrasts. A variety of grass-leaved plants helps create a sense of place through their distribution around the garden. The fine texture of their blades is echoed on the upper plane, and all of this feathered delicacy contrasts pleasantly with the large-leaved plants, such as the hydrangeas and rhododendron. Add to this the medium textures and various colors of the other foliage and flowers, and the result is a garden that is never the same from one moment to the next and that offers no end of visual interest.

This garden's measure of success is the degree to which it gladdens its owner, who looks forward to getting up in the morning and coming home every day just to spend time in it. The garden provides her pleasant anticipation and daily happiness. It is also a dramatic addition to the neighborhood streetscape, with more than one neighbor altering her morning route just to witness this riotous suburban spree. Too few suburban gardens step out of the stereotype to provide these enjoyments.

Lessons from a Small Garden

Design theme
The elevated foundation and the owner's wish for color and abundance were the motivating impulses behind this garden's design. *(top left)*

Organization of space
Two terracing walls create three tiers, primarily to provide dimensionality, interest, and gracefulness. *(top right)*

Structure
Textured concrete walls offset the abundant planting. *(middle left)*

Boundary structure
None, as this is a front yard.

Combination of materials
Rich combination of textural contrasts and harmonies in conjunction with the lawn and walls creates a satisfying look. *(middle right and bottom left)*

Proportion
More apparent in winter, the height of the walls is about one-third the length of the space in front of them. *(top right)*

Details
Three tiers give complexity; the curving lines of walls, lawn, and beds add gracefulness. The two-level water garden provides considerable interest, as do the intense contrasts and harmonies in the lush planting scheme. *(bottom right)*

Garden of Peacefulness

Creating an Organic Environment

**Complexity
Level 2**

Garden size:
16 feet wide × 22 feet deep
(4.9 meters wide × 6.7 meters deep)

Raised beds, a curvy fieldstone wall, a corner water garden, and lush plantings combine to add interest and expansion in this small rectangular garden. Gone is the instantaneous apprehension of the space, replaced by a visual exploration excited into action by pleasing line and intricacy of detail.

This garden suffered poor spatial organization, with a small central living area and narrow beds all around. In addition, it was dark and cold—the consequence of a large Ailanthus tree. Small gardens may feel even smaller and completely unwelcoming when the accessible areas are too small. Though the space may be 22 feet by 16 feet (4.9 m × 6.7 m), if no accommodation is made for human activities other than tending plants, if no outdoor living is to be had, people will not want to be in the garden. In this case, the restrictiveness plus the darkness made the place feel quite uninviting.

Above: A typical urban backyard before transformation.

A lush planting of diverse species is unified through repeating foliar qualities and similarities in plant groupings.

Small Garden · Wisdom	**Follow these guidelines when designing a lush, natural garden:**
	✹ Use curves to elicit a sense of organic motion.
	✹ Exploit fieldstone's unmanufactured nature when even a hint of formality is inappropriate.
	✹ Repeat leaf forms, colors, and combinations thereof to express unity in the garden.

Curves Elicit a Sense of Organic Motion

Not only is the division of space critical, the line those divisions define is too. This is especially apparent in small gardens, where virtually every component makes a significant contribution as either an asset or a detriment. The shortest distance between two points is a straight line visually as well as physically. When a small space is organized along straight lines, as was the case here, everything is seen at once. The eye doesn't traverse the length of a line but goes immediately to its termination and takes no joy in the journey—in fact, doesn't even seem to have made one. The environment is static and the space seems dimensionless. This garden cried out for flowing motion, for warmth, light, and life.

The owners of this garden were clearly possessed of a deep appreciation of the natural. They wanted to generate in it an organic feel that would remind them of their lush homeland, Nicaragua, while providing them the ability to entertain small groups. Being active businesspeople with high-pressure responsibilities, they also wanted a garden that invited private, peaceful contemplation while offering the options of outdoor living—all within a very small space.

Terracing was chosen here partially for practical purposes. The giant ailanthus tree did a wonderful job of screening neighboring buildings, but it cast too much shade, and its roots filled the garden. Thinning it would mitigate the shade sufficiently, but nothing would be able to grow without raised beds. In addition to providing good planting areas, a raised bed would also provide another dimension to the garden, and consequently, a sense of expansion. Given that parameter, the question was how to open the space and vivify it with the qualities the owners craved.

To break up the static, linear aspect, the main living area was scooped out in curvy, organic fashion. To accentuate the organic effect, fieldstone was chosen as the retaining material and laid without mortar.

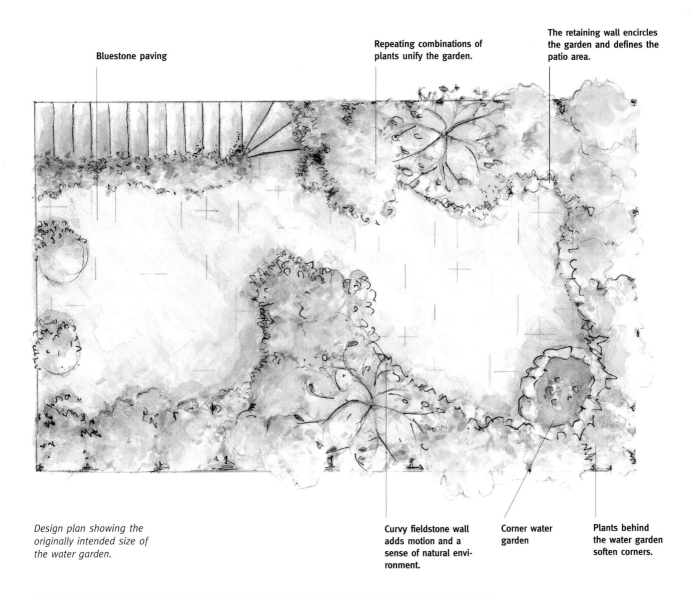

Bluestone paving

Repeating combinations of plants unify the garden.

The retaining wall encircles the garden and defines the patio area.

Design plan showing the originally intended size of the water garden.

Curvy fieldstone wall adds motion and a sense of natural environment.

Corner water garden

Plants behind the water garden soften corners.

Fear Not Elements of Interest

THE MORE ELEMENTS OF INTEREST A GARDEN CONTAINS, THE MORE SATISFYING EXPERIENCES THE VISITOR CAN HAVE AND THE LESS LIMITING THE GARDEN'S SMALL SIZE. KEEP IN MIND THAT THESE ELEMENTS SHOULD ALL RELATE WELL TO ONE ANOTHER. TOO MUCH UNRELATED DIVERSITY STRIKES THE EYE AS CLUTTER AND IS CONSTRICTING. SO IS TOO MUCH OPENNESS, TOO FEW ELEMENTS WITH WHICH TO CONNECT. YOU CAN FEEL CLOSED OFF IN A DESERT BECAUSE OF THE APPARENT LACK OF DETAIL, WHEREAS AN ABUNDANCE OF INTERESTING ELEMENTS, WELL INTEGRATED, STIMULATE AND EXPAND THE EXPERIENCE AND ENLARGE THE SENSE OF SPACE. YOU CAN EXPERIENCE A SMALL, WELL-MADE GARDEN AS UNENDING, GIVEN A RICH TAPESTRY OF PLANTS IN APPEALING COMBINATION, ROCKS IN PLEASING GROUPINGS, A VARIETY OF PLANES THE EYE CAN TRAVERSE, OR OTHER ELEMENTS THAT ATTRACT AND PLEASE.

Choose Fieldstone for a Natural Environment

Notice that the final design of this garden is similar to that of the first garden featured (page 12) and contains significant elements found in the garden on page 36, yet the final effect is quite different. Why is that? Materials. These examples dramatically demonstrate the importance of materials for generating specific effects.

Natural stone is one of the few building materials that utterly lacks a manufactured aspect. Even brick, which is nothing more than baked earth, introduces a civilized and formal quality due to its relative uniformity. In the garden on page 12, brick was chosen as a tame material with a suburban, familiar feel that was suited to the family the garden was built for. In addition, the brick provided a structure and surface amenable to the children's use. The concrete interlocking blocks featured on page 36 adapted well to the given budget and suited the suburban nature of the neighborhood.

Fieldstone, on the other hand, is completely natural and can be used to heighten the sense of a natural environment. When walls of stone are built without mortar, the ultimate degree of earthiness can be achieved within a stable, functional structure, especially as plants begin to make their homes in the nooks and crannies.

The curved wall creates a line the eye wants to follow, generating a sense of motion and interest as well as softening and relaxing the space. One's attention is at first swept along this curve, but it leaps at various points to different views the garden offers.

The wall also supports a water garden in the far right corner. Note, however, that it is not quite in the corner. A small space was left behind it for plants. Without the plants, that portion of the garden would seem and, in fact, be much harder, especially with the river stone/fieldstone wall from which the water issues as it trickles into the pool below.

Welcome Friends with a Natural Arbor

The design plan for this garden shows the planting on the right sweeping outward toward the entry stairs and the planting in the raised bed on the left leaning in toward the center. This creates a natural arbor as the entry to the garden—a wonderful element to include whenever possible. We all enjoy the feeling of actual entry into a pleasant place, and especially a garden. A slight moment of hesitation, a tiny element of suspense as we cross from our ordinary world beneath a leafy bower into a foliage- and flower-filled garden, is simply delightful.

Above and opposite: Flowing water, swimming fish, and water plants bring an aqueous world to the terrestrial garden.

Add Dimension with Water Gardens

DON'T THINK THAT A SMALL SPACE IS TOO SMALL FOR A WATER GARDEN—THAT TOO MUCH AREA IS LOST THAT COULD OTHERWISE BE PLANTED OR USED FOR A TABLE OR CHAIRS. IN FACT, WATER GARDENS ADD SPACE BY ADDING INTEREST. ANY ELEMENT THAT DRAWS THE ATTENTION OF THE SENSES HAS THE EFFECT OF EXPANDING AND PROLONGING ONE'S EXPERIENCE OF THE GARDEN—THEREBY ENLARGING IT. WATER GARDENS ARE EXCELLENT FOR THIS. THE DELIGHTFUL SOUND OF CASCADING WATER, REFLECTIONS ON A PLACID POOL, THE COLORS AND MOTION OF SWIMMING FISH, DAY- AND NIGHT-BLOOMING WATER LILIES— FEW OTHER ELEMENTS OFFER SO MUCH IN SO LITTLE SPACE.

Mix and Match Leaves for Lush Foliage

Perhaps the outstanding attribute of this garden is how wonderfully lush it is. The wealth of textures, the countless shades and colors of the leaves, the many plant forms all provide richness and diversity. Yet this garden does not feel busy or eclectic. Why is that? It is the quality of unity resulting from the principle of repetition. Here, not only are individual leaf and plant forms repeated, but so are similar combinations of plants.

For example, the bold leaf and broad form of the hydrangea contrasts superbly with the variegated iris while the variegations of both harmonize. This theme of harmony-contrast combinations is carried on in smaller scale with the variegated dwarf berberis in combination with variegated liriope and in even smaller scale in the variegated leaves of euonymous and thyme.

These groupings transition into the dark, glossy-leaved ilex, creating a vivid foliar contrast while a twig dogwood picks up the variegation theme and deepens the contrast element by its relation to the nearby holly. Below them, the glossy gaultheria echoes the holly while contrasting with the liriope.

The grassy leaves of iris and ornamental grasses in contrast with bold-leaved plants, the sedum that spill over the wall here and there, and the vines throughout bind the garden, forming a complex tapestry while uniting it into a diverse yet singular place. There is no end of detail to attract and please the eye, yet the garden has the quality of peacefulness the owners sought.

A lush sanctuary belies its urban setting.

Lessons from a Small Garden

Design theme
The homeowner's desire for a natural, serene sanctuary. *(top left)*

Organization of space
A single retaining wall wraps through the property, defining the patio area, the raised beds, and water garden. *(top right)*

Structure
The stone wall and water garden are the primary structural elements. *(middle left)*

Boundary structure
An existing fence was left in place, as it is weathered and contributes to the desired qualities. *(middle right)*

Combination of materials
New York bluestone with Pennsylvania fieldstone harmonize with one another and work well with plants. *(bottom left)*

Proportion
The patio is as large as could be accommodated without making the raised areas too small. The water garden was made larger than the original plan called for at the owner's request and occupies a disproportionate amount of space. However, because it is defined by the continuous retaining wall and sustains plant life, it works. *(top left and bottom right)*

Summary of Details
As the structural elements are fairly simple, they serve as an excellent backdrop for the diverse planting scheme.

Enlarging the Garden through Division

In this chapter we begin to explore how to enlarge a small space through division. It is natural to think that dividing a small space will make it seem even smaller but, in fact, the reverse is often the case. If properly done, dividing a space can make the garden feel considerably larger than the sum of its areas, as long as each area is ample enough to invite use or appears purposeful. It is as if we sense that, "Well, here we are in a garden and it is a pleasant place to be, and right over there is another garden area, and it is inviting." This quality of an invitation to explore what seems to be another entire garden plays an important part in divided gardens, whether a physical or a visual exploration is offered.

Garden divisions can be so complete as to create two or more distinct garden rooms by the use of arbors and structures. Merely carving out of the main area smaller, slightly separated spaces can expand the garden. More subtle divisions created by defining spaces through the use of different materials—for example, stone blending into water or water to lawn or lawn to beach pebbles—can expand the perceived area. In these latter instances, each area defined by a distinct material must be large enough in itself to sustain its reason for being and sufficiently integrated with the rest of the garden through, for example, form and line, to sustain the overall unity.

Victorian Garden Rooms

Blending Ornament with Nature

Complexity Level 4

Garden size:
16 feet wide × 60 feet deep
(4.9 meters wide × 18.3 meters deep)

This small garden, of a very definite quality and richness, was hiding behind bad planning, poor construction, and neglect. Though full of potential, the site seemed much too narrow and was exceedingly gloomy and still. It wanted life and action, movement and light. Especially, it wanted to be restored to that era of Victorian elegance it was originally intended to embody.

Rich in the darker sides of the Victorian epic, the garden hinted of intrigue and mystery, evoking a sense of secret passages, romance, and ornament. However, the garden was only partially developed and long neglected. Fine old rhododendrons and azaleas arched over a tumbledown wall. A mature flowering cherry in the rear cast deep shadows across the entire width, while a shaggy and diseased hemlock hedge bordered the long street-side axis. Two forlorn cedars added an air of mystery—but their placement was unfortunate. They segmented the long axis in just the wrong place, making the area near the garden entrance cramped and dark while encroaching on the remaining space, making the space seem tiny.

Above: The garden before transformation, seen from the front looking toward the rear.

Victorian romance in three parts.

Small Garden Wisdom	**Bring grace to a long strip of a garden by following these guidelines:** ❋ Segment a narrow garden into rooms to make it seem more spacious. ❋ Seek the alternatives hiding in apparently all-or-nothing solutions. ❋ Express the unity of garden rooms with repeated materials and plants.

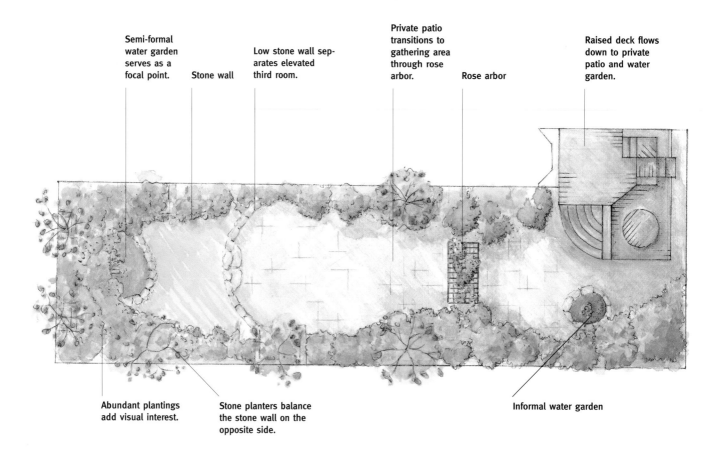

Semi-formal water garden serves as a focal point.

Stone wall

Low stone wall separates elevated third room.

Private patio transitions to gathering area through rose arbor.

Rose arbor

Raised deck flows down to private patio and water garden.

Abundant plantings add visual interest.

Stone planters balance the stone wall on the opposite side.

Informal water garden

Above: The design plan.

The interior of the home had been tastefully reconstructed in the Victorian tradition, and it was important to maintain those same qualities in the garden. Thus, there needed to be a blend of man-made with organic—a wedding of nature with ornament in a setting that was, overall, romantic in its feel and effect.

It is best, especially with long-neglected sites, to begin by dealing with the negative elements. The cedars had to go, being too large for transplanting. The retaining wall tumbling out 4 feet (1.2 m) from the side of the home had to be rebuilt closer to the house, capturing a precious 2 feet (.6 m) of garden width, and the cherry had to be pruned. By opening both the sky and the sides this way, the garden could gain both air and breadth.

Look Beyond the Obvious Solutions

The sparsely branched and scale-infested hemlock hedge raised several questions. A double-paneled lattice privacy fence planted in vines was planned, so the hedge wasn't essential as a screen, but removal was costly and potentially problematic, as the roots had certainly grown beneath the existing iron picket fence foundation. If properly pruned, the hedge might become a rich textural element as well as contributing as an additional screen. But the question was not, as it happened, an all-or-nothing proposition, and this reveals an important aspect of the design process.

It is sometimes advantageous to look between the solutions, next to the apparent possibilities, for more subtle resolutions of design problems. In this instance, both removing and keeping the hemlock hedge had advantages and disadvantages. Looking between these two apparent choices, it became obvious that the best approach was to keep most of the hemlock, prune and treat for scale, removing some in groups of two along the length of the hedge. Stone planters were set in the resulting spaces, which balanced the stone wall on the opposite side of the yard and provided growing areas for vines to cover the lattice and for trees and shrubs to grow without competition from hemlock roots.

Discover and Define Garden Rooms

Once the yard was opened, deepened, and given breadth, its possibilities became clear. The narrow lengthiness of the property, accentuated by the height of the building, called for division into a series of garden rooms, one leading into another. If left undivided, the site would have had ample length but would have seemed constricted because of its unbalanced proportions. It would also have remained static and, therefore, not have invited use. Dividing the garden into three distinct garden rooms eliminated the sense of narrowness. It added intrigue in the invitation from room to room. It generated a sense of expansiveness by blurring the boundaries of the garden. From nowhere can the limits of the garden be discerned.

Divide a Long Space into Rooms

A LONG EXPANSE IS FINE FOR PUBLIC PLACES THAT MUST ACCOMMODATE MANY PEOPLE AT ONCE, IF THERE ARE ACTIVE CHILDREN AT HOME, OR ON AN ESTATE WHOSE GARDEN BOASTS MANY OTHER USABLE PORTIONS, BUT FOR PRIVATE USE, CONSIDER DIVIDING A LONG SPACE INTO USABLE ROOMS TO ACCOMMODATE NATURAL AND PRACTICAL USE. THE AREA CAN THEN OFFER MANY MORE POSSIBILITIES AND BE MADE TO SEEM MUCH ROOMIER, DISPELLING THE OPPRESSIVE SENSE OF CONFINEMENT THAT OFTEN DOMINATES LONG, NARROW SITES.

The area closest the house entry is composed of a redwood deck that flows easily down to an intimate patio containing an informal water garden and an abundance of graceful plantings. This room is meant to give the owners an easily accessible deck and garden where they can take in the long view of their garden, enjoy a private meal, a cup of coffee, or glass of wine, or just break from their daily routine in a lovely garden environment. As the deck is off the kitchen and the garden below a few steps farther, this area serves as the primary outdoor family room.

The family room is separated from the second area by a wide arbor that permits an easy view into the second and third garden rooms. The second garden room is the largest. It adds considerably to the overall sense of spaciousness this landscape now conveys because one moves from an intimate though ample deck and patio area into a yet more spacious area with a view into still another chamber of the garden. This experience of motion, of expansion through space, creates a sense of amplitude.

One division creating two garden rooms would have been sufficient to maximize the available space, but the yard easily supported three areas. The additional division would enhance interest and the sense of possibility. The other motive for creating a third area was the downward slope of the yard. Terracing was a natural treatment for a portion of the garden, while the remaining section could simply be divided by an arbor and plants.

View of the garden from the deck.

Making Inviting Spaces Near the Home Entry

PEOPLE NATURALLY USE GARDEN AREAS NEAREST THE ENTRY CONSIDERABLY MORE THAN THE MORE REMOTE SPACES. WHEN BUILDING EVEN A SMALL GARDEN, IT IS IMPORTANT TO CREATE ENJOYABLE SPACES CLOSE TO THE POINT OF ENTRANCE SO THAT THE INHABITANTS, IN THEIR BUSY DAY, WILL TAKE THE TIME TO ENTER THE GARDEN AND DELIGHT IN IT.

View of the garden from the informal patio off the deck.

Above left: Repetition of forms, as in the retaining wall and the wall of the water garden, creates harmonies. The same arching line is to be found in the stone planters and the arbor.

Above right: The formal water garden in the third section of the garden.

Opposite: View looking toward the front of the garden.

The third garden room is elevated and separated from the second by a low stone wall. Proportion here is important. If too tall, the wall would have the effect of a barrier, inhibiting forward motion. If too low, it would seem foolish and unnecessary. As it is, it lifts the eye, carrying one's vision to some remote point, undeterminable because of the abundant plantings at the rear of the garden. This area also invites the visitor, contributing to the experience of motion through space.

Central to the third partition is the semiformal water garden, which serves several functions. An ornament in itself, it sits like a jewel in its verdant surroundings, providing visual and audio interest as well as masking street noises. In addition, the water feature serves as a focal point from the very front of the garden, drawing one's attention from the deck through the entire expanse of the landscape as one enters it.

Tying It All Together

Though the garden, in keeping with the Victorian tradition, abounds with diversity, two primary elements weld these three rooms into a single environment: the use of stone throughout and the repetition of form. Stone planters on the left balance with the dry-laid stone wall on the right and rear, while the curves of the arbor, the rear retaining wall, the planters, and the water garden wall help integrate each area into a consistent whole. A site that once seemed confining now invites and expands, offering myriad possibilities of enjoyment within a motif of Victorian romance.

Invite Use by Creating Level Surfaces

EVEN A GENTLE SLOPE IS TIRING, BOTH MENTALLY AND PHYSICALLY. ANY AREA TO BE USED OTHER THAN AS A TRANSITION FROM ONE PLACE TO ANOTHER SHOULD BE LEVEL. FLAT PLANES ARE RESTFUL, INVITING, AND PLEASING, BOTH AESTHETICALLY AND PRACTICALLY. THIS IS ESPECIALLY TRUE WHEN THEY ARE COVERED IN A UNIFORM SURFACE, WHETHER STONE, GRASS, OR ANY OTHER MATERIAL.

Lessons from a Small Garden

Design theme
Victorian elements permeated the place and set the theme for the garden's development, arrived at by removing the negative, then enhancing the positive romantic qualities with a balance of ornament in natural materials.

Organization of space
One space was divided into three interconnected garden rooms.

Structure
The redwood deck is a substantial structure that anchors the entire garden at that end. At the other end is the formal Victorian water garden. Between is the wood arbor, a low stone wall, and the stone patio. These combine to create ornament in natural materials—a characteristic of the Victorian style—while contributing to the garden's functionality.

Boundary structure
Lattice panels, a hemlock hedge, and stone planters border the garden on one side and are balanced by the building on the other.

Combination of materials
Stone and wood are the primary materials throughout, both ornamented and softened with flowers and foliage.

Proportion
Each room needed to be large enough for use without making any other seem small. It was important for the walls to be of proper height in relation to both their length and the depth of the area behind them. The side retaining wall could be higher because the space behind it was meant only as a home for plants.

Summary of Details
The two water gardens, dry-laid walls, and stone planters add a textural richness and natural elegance. The planting is luxuriant and informal within a tightly structured organization of space, creating a balanced contrast.

A Tranquil Elegance

Exploring Textures and Graceful Curves

Complexity Level 3

Garden size:
16 feet wide × 22 feet deep
(4.9 meters wide × 6.7 meters deep)

Although enlarging a garden by division usually implies one area separated from another by a definite structure, a subtler method of creating a sense of expansion through division is to juxtapose highly contrasting materials.

For a sense of harmony, balance, and unity, create areas that mimic each other in size and, especially, in shape. In this small garden, the curving line of the round patio provides a graceful element, while the line of its upper arch is echoed through the water garden, lawn, and pebble beach. The repetition of line brings a unifying harmony, while the contrasts in textures expand the experience of the garden visually and tactilely.

Above: The garden before transformation.

The repetition of curves lends a sense of grace and unity to the transformed garden.

The Dynmics of Diagonals

DIAGONAL LINES CAN OFTEN BE USED EFFECTIVELY IN GARDEN DESIGN, ESPECIALLY WHERE MOTION AND ACTION ARE WANTED. HOWEVER, BEAR IN MIND THAT THEIR USE MUST BE CAREFULLY CONTROLLED, AS THE FINAL EFFECT CAN EASILY BECOME FRENETICALLY BUSY. HERE, A DIAGONALLY PATTERNED LATTICE FENCE WOULD HAVE DESTROYED THE SENSE OF PEACE THE OWNERS SOUGHT FOR THEIR GARDEN.

Small Garden — Wisdom

Instill harmony and order in a small garden with these ideas:

* Create divisions through the use of contrasting materials.
* Exploit the tactile values of contrasting materials by placing them in close proximity.
* Create harmony between contrasting divisions by repeating them.

Before redesign, this tiny space was not only void of pleasing elements but also ridden with disagreeable components. The chain-link fence imbued the place with a prisonlike quality, the ubiquitous Ivy was invasive, and the raised platform, when used, made the owners feel exposed and confined—when not, it seemed purposeless. The small concrete patio area was functional but graceless. The only sense of garden came from the large Pear tree in the rear and the Grapevine growing on the fence to the right.

Seek Order and Harmony in Building a Sanctuary

As professionals in high-pressure occupations, the owners needed a peaceful sanctuary in which they could remove themselves from their daily toil and find meaning and satisfaction in a natural world. This urban tangle, before remaking, was the opposite. The confused conglomeration of discordant ingredients created a patchwork of useless areas and, in fact, the theme of the site seemed to be confusion itself. The place called out for order and harmony. It needed to be freed of its oppressive quality, separated from the surrounding world, and instilled with meaning and serenity. Therein spoke the genius. The place desperately wanted a harmonious composition of recognizable forms and pleasing materials, within an expanding framework—separated from the outside world but not confining.

Wed Strength with Delicacy to Generate Tranquility

Rather than attempt to obscure the boundaries with an indefinite structure and an abundance of plantings, as was done in the garden on page 14, the owners sought a precise definition of the garden space in order to generate a sense of tranquility through separation from the outer world. Yet, particularly given the smallness of the space, too solid a fence would have been oppressive and anything too busy, distracting. Anything too light would have created a sense of vulnerability. This thick cedar lattice with square rather than diagonal boxes ensures privacy without confining or distracting. It accentuates the quality of sedate elegance found throughout the garden.

Above and right: A thick cedar lattice encloses the garden with a masculine form.

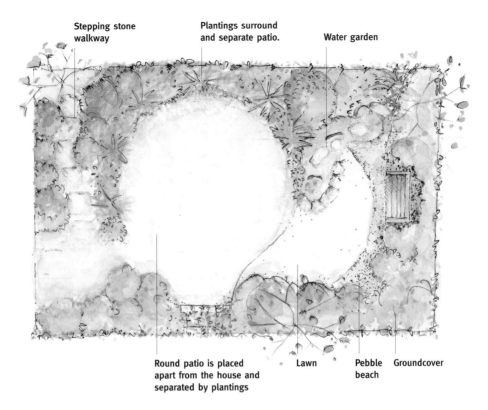

Stepping stone walkway

Plantings surround and separate patio.

Water garden

Round patio is placed apart from the house and separated by plantings

Lawn

Pebble beach

Groundcover

Because the owners were friendly with the neighbors on the right, that side of the fence was kept low and an arbor with a gate was built in. This did not cause a sense of imbalance because the garden is not bilaterally symmetrical between any two points. The arbor, covered in grapevine, lends an element of mystery and dimension to the garden, and the lowness of that side adds a friendly note. Finally, the lattice fence provides a richly textured and consistent backdrop, binding the garden and bringing it into focus, much as a picture frame does a picture.

Exploit Masculine and Feminine Forms

Within this secure, masculine framework, the garden needed to be defined as a soothing and serene place. Round and curving forms are feminine and convey the sense of softness and gentleness called for here. A round patio sounded the keynote and its form influenced everything surrounding it, imparting its graceful, feminine quality to the rest.

Make the Patio a Garden Room, Not an Outdoor House Room

The original patio was of thin tiles on concrete, built right up to the house and had a 60s look to it. This was taken up, and a new patio was built of New York stone on stone dust. This patio, satisfying to look at by virtue of its shape and size, was placed away from the house and separated from it by plantings. This is almost always the best approach to patio placement, though not always easy in a small garden. A patio surrounded with plantings belongs to the garden; a patio attached to a building is dominated by the building. Here, a simple stepping-stone walkway between plantings leads from the house to the patio, set slightly apart from the walk to accentuate its round form. The path itself has interest and intent in that it is built, in part, with large heirloom tiles bearing oriental characters meaningful to the owners.

Diversity in a Small Garden

It cannot be overstated how important unity of place is, even in the small garden, yet how necessary diversity is, especially in a small garden. The repetition of line through different media creates unity through form and, at the same time, provides contrasts in texture. The curving line of this patio ripples through the lawn and water garden, the pebble beach, and groundcover planting beyond. These contrasting elements create different spaces, or divisions, that stand out from one another, and it is this that contributes to the sense of expansion. Four distinct areas are visible, each of which can be accessed, yet together they form a unity of form.

Keep Garden Elements in Mutual Proportion

The patio, the water garden, the lawn, pebble beach, and the plantings needed to be proportional to each other. The fence needed to be in proportion to these and to the outer world. (The patio, for example, makes the fence seem large, while the neighboring buildings make it seem small.) Though the garden is bold in its well-defined forms, it is delicate in its proportions—and, in such a tiny space, it had to be. Had any of the components been too large or small, it would have failed, and the garden as a whole would have failed.

The most notable characteristic of this completed garden is that it is clearly a designed environment in which everything makes sense in itself and in relation to what is around it. All the initial confusion deriving from the arbitrary combination of components has been removed and the inherent serenity of the place revealed and developed.

Above: The quintessential quality of a garden is life. A water garden profoundly enhances this quality.

Right: Well-defined forms with recurring shapes help generate a sophisticated sense of place.

Harmonies and Contrasts

AN IMPORTANT PRINCIPLE IN ALL DESIGN—CREATE HARMONIES AND CONTRASTS—DERIVES FROM OUR EMOTIONAL RESPONSE TO PERCEIVED RELATIONSHIPS AMONG OBJECTS. IF TWO ELEMENTS DO NOT HARMONIZE OR CONTRAST NOTICEABLY, IF THEY HAVE NO PERCEIVED RELATIONSHIP TO ONE ANOTHER, THEN THEIR COMBINATION DOES NOT AFFECT US—AND THEY SHOULD NOT BE COMBINED.

SOMETIMES WE ENJOY CONTRASTS, AS IN OPPOSITE COLOR COMBINATIONS—REDS WITH BLUES—AND DIFFERENT TEXTURES—GRASS AND STONE. HARMONIES ARE AT OTHER TIMES MORE SATISFYING AND ARE ESSENTIAL IN CREATING THE ALL-IMPORTANT QUALITY OF UNITY. UNITING TWO OR MORE ELEMENTS THROUGH BOTH HARMONIES AND CONTRASTS, FOR EXAMPLE, A HARMONY OF FORM AND CONTRAST OF TEXTURE OR COLOR, EVOKES THE MOST PLEASING AND EMPHATIC RESPONSE.

Lessons from a Small Garden

Design theme
This space had been so badly developed that it demanded its opposite. The calm nature of the clients and the fact of their high-pressure occupations helped the design approach solidify around a concept of well-defined forms, carefully controlled and interrelated.

Organization of space
The divisions between the areas are by material only. Patio ripples into water and into lawn, which seamlessly adjoins a pebble beach laced by a planting of groundcover. These divisions are visually perceived and palpably felt.

Structure
The patio and the water garden, along with the existing pear tree, are the only interior structures. In this small space, they are enough to balance with the foliage and blossoms.

Boundary structure
The cedar lattice fence has square openings, giving a tranquil, elegant effect. Carried through three sides, it helps unify the garden. The fence is lower on one neighbor's side, and an arbor with a gate connects the two gardens.

Combination of materials
Stone and water, lawn and beach pebbles, plants and wood all combine through the principles of harmony and contrast.

Proportion
The patio is large enough for easy use and is prominent in the garden without overpowering it. Each of the other distinct areas—the water garden, the lawn, the beach, and the planting beds—exist in delicate, proportional harmony with one another and within the whole.

Summary of Details
The square lattice fence supporting flowering vines adds considerable detail, as does the flow of form through the different media of the patio, water garden, lawn, beach, and surrounding plantings.

Friendly Yet Sophisticated Garden

Balancing Style with Function

**Complexity
Level 2**

Garden size:
16 feet wide × 30 feet deep
(4.9 meters wide × 9.1 meters deep)

This small garden shows how both structural and textural elements contribute to the creation of divisions that appear to enlarge the available space. Compare this technique to previous methods of division: dividing a small garden into three separate rooms by the strong use of structure alone (page 54) and dividing simply by the use of different materials (page 62).

The simple iron arbor, (quickly enveloped with yellow and white climbing roses), creates a vertical boundary between the two primary areas while the transition from stone to grass further heightens the sense of two distinct rooms. There is no elevation change between the two primary spaces, yet this simple arbor and surface change create a definite division. It is not necessary to use the arbor to pass from one area into the other— a stepping stone path leads up the right side, connecting the patio to the shed. Nevertheless, the ample patio and passage through the arbor to the garden area beyond contributes considerably to a sense of spaciousness. A third area to the very rear, a raised bed retained by a stone wall, lifts the termination of the garden into another dimension, furthering the sense and, in fact, the reality of space.

*Above: An old-time back-
yard garden with lawn
and shrubbery, neither
interesting nor enjoyable.*

Diagonal placement of the arbor and curves off the angles in the patio bring a touch of sophistication to this welcoming layout.

Small Garden ———●——— Wisdom	**Apply these ideas to increase movement and ease in a static garden space:**
	❋ Exploit both structural and textural elements to create divisions in the garden. ❋ Relax a rectangular garden space with curved rather than straight-edged planting beds. ❋ Use an arbor as a vertical divider between garden rooms, even if it is not over the only route between them.

Although the original layout of this garden was friendly enough—the sort of backyard one's grandmother may have had—it lacked both grace and a sense of style. Most of the elements the owners wanted—lawn, patio, and planting beds—were present, but they expressed no plan or design and were not particularly attractive. The planting beds went straight up the sides, the components did not cooperate with each other, and the whole lacked composition. One area abruptly joined another in static disregard.

Seek the Genius in Both Garden and Gardeners

The final design for the garden evolved from three factors:

1. a modification of the owners' concept, which showed a taste for curves as well as for rectangular patterns and natural materials
2. the owners themselves, who exhibited a quiet reserve and a friendly European sophistication
3. the innate possibilities of the place—the raised area in the rear; the long, flat yard; the Old-World shrubbery

Below: The modified design plan.

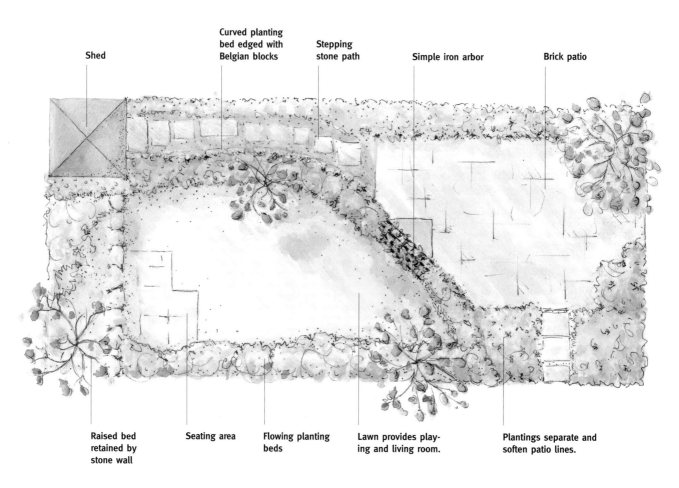

Shed

Curved planting bed edged with Belgian blocks

Stepping stone path

Simple iron arbor

Brick patio

Raised bed retained by stone wall

Seating area

Flowing planting beds

Lawn provides playing and living room.

Plantings separate and soften patio lines.

At the same time, practicality called for play areas for two small children, and, to support the owners' devotion to gardening, a shed for garden tools. All these factors led to a theme suited to the owners and with which the site seemed in harmony—a nicely shaped and placed patio transitioning into a lawn area bordered by flowing, not static beds and containing a Belgian block-delineated planting bed. At the rear of the property was a raised bed retained by fieldstone. Beside that was the garden shed with a footpath back to the patio.

Push Beyond the First Sketch to Amplify the Design

Taken as a whole, this design provided a slightly sophisticated though unpretentious garden endowed with ample interest, considerable functionality, and a natural friendliness. But just how does one create friendliness in a garden? And what constitutes sophistication? How does one endow a garden with those aesthetic and emotional qualities? How does one control the quantity of those ephemeral endowments, keeping the garden from being too styled or too easygoing? This is what garden design is all about, and it really is not all that mysterious.

Both the owner's sketch and the final design contain essentially the same elements: a patio and lawn, a Belgium block-edged bed, a pathway to the rear, a shed, a rear seating area, and a raised bed. The sketch, however, offers just a basic definition of spaces. The patio is a simple rectangle, the lawn area is an amorphous blob, and the planting areas are straight up the sides with little flow toward the center. To the rear is a narrow bed retained by a low wall. The design lacks sophistication, and with the patio placed squarely against the neighboring structures and with the entire space open and exposed, the design lacks the quality of warmth.

How to Create a Mood

TO CREATE A QUALITY SUCH AS FRIENDLINESS, SOPHISTICATION, EXCITEMENT, OR REPOSE, BEGIN BY ANALYZING WHAT THAT QUALITY REALLY SPECIFIES. EXCITEMENT, FOR EXAMPLE, ALWAYS INVOLVES RAPID CHANGE OR UNEXPECTED ELEMENTS OR THE ENCOUNTERING OF DANGER, THE DRAMATIC, OR THE UNPREDICTABLE. THE NEXT STEP IS TO IDENTIFY THE PHYSICAL ELEMENTS THAT EVOKE THESE RESPONSES.

FRIENDLINESS ARISES FROM THE SOFTNESS, HARMONY, WARMTH, AND FAMILIARITY THAT MAKE A PLACE ACCOMMODATING AND INVITING. SOPHISTICATION IMPLIES A SENSE OF STYLE EXHIBITED THROUGH THE LINES OF A COMPOSITION AND THE RELATIONSHIPS OF ITS COMPONENTS, USUALLY WITH SOME DEGREE OF COMPLEXITY. FOR EXAMPLE, WHEN AN ELEMENT SUCH AS A DIAGONAL LINE IS REPEATED THROUGH DIFFERENT MEDIA OR ON HIGHER OR LOWER SCALES, THE SCENE IS ENDOWED WITH A GREATER DEGREE OF DESIGN COMPLEXITY, CONVEYING A SENSE OF SOPHISTICATION. A BRICK WALL IS RICHER AND MORE SOPHISTICATED THAN A PLAIN FENCE. WITH A BUILT-IN ARCH, THE WALL TAKES ON A GREATER DEGREE OF DESIGN COMPLEXITY AND BECOMES YET MORE SOPHISTICATED. ADD A LION-HEAD FOUNTAIN AND CLOTHE IT IN A FLOWERING VINE TO YIELD A SCENE RICH IN DESIGNED, HARMONIOUS DETAILS AND A HIGH DEGREE OF SOPHISTICATION.

Pennisetum, anemone, and
rosa rubrifolia blend fine, bold,
and medium textures.

In the final design plan, the patio's somewhat more sophisticated design is still in keeping with the rectilinear preferences of the owners, but it integrates better with the lawn and is pulled away from the enclosing structures so that plantings can separate it from the house. This treatment softens the borders, introducing elements of style and of friendliness. The diagonal line of the patio's front edge is carried through the Belgium block-edged planting bed, adding a graceful touch. The bed then arches, defining in soft curves the outer line of the lawn. The rear seating area is now in the far left corner and indented. In conjunction with the retaining wall behind it, it balances with and reflects the main patio while forming a triangular relationship with the main patio and the tool shed.

The abundant plantings, which flow into the lawn area, embrace the patio, and fill the enlarged rear raised bed, generate the quality of friendliness with their informal abundance, as does the curved planting bed filled with graceful ornamental grasses and red-leaved roses.

Above: The arbor invites the visitor to explore the garden.

Left: A brick wall with built-in arch and lion-head fountain bring a touch of European sophistication to the garden.

Diagonal Lines Radiate Energy

USE DIAGONALS FOR EXCITEMENT AND MOTION. IN CONTRAST, RIGHT ANGLES, AS FOUND IN RECTANGLES AND SQUARES, COUNTERBALANCE EACH OTHER AND ARE STATIC. DIAGONALS WORK WITH THE PERPENDICULAR LINES, EXTENDING THEIR INFLUENCE RATHER THAN CANCELING THEM OUT.

The simple iron arbor adds a touch of style as well as warmth, which will be enhanced as yellow and white climbing roses begin to cover it. It is an appealing element in itself and seems to invite the visitor to explore the garden beyond. Placed on the diagonal, the arbor adds interest and motion, dispelling the static quality that rectangular spaces often project. It creates a vertical boundary between the two primary areas, reinforcing the sense of two distinct rooms expressed by the transition from stone to grass.

The cedar lattice panels, regularly spaced along both side boundaries, add a touch of warmth and sophistication. The brick wall, whose built-in arch containing a lion-head fountain adds both a natural warmth and a European element, also contributes to the garden's quality of sophistication.

Do Design Exercises for Fun and Learning

Above: Variegated hydrangea blends well with ferns, bleeding heart, and aak-leaf hydrangea.

Below: The family rabbit romps through the garden.

Either of these qualities, warm friendliness and sophistication, could have been developed further. For example, if a greater degree of sophistication had been desired, the patio could have been given a more complex form with angles in the corners, by rounding the upper right end, or by enclosing it in a brick wall on the two long sides and partially across the front. Given the neighborhood and the needs and the tastes of the owners, however, this would have been too much and would have undermined the desired sense of ease and congeniality.

A more easygoing quality could have been achieved by bringing the plantings further into the lawn area in curvy, alternating beds, by lessening the amount of paved area, and by replacing more of the lawn and shed in the rear with planting beds. This would have cut into the desired quality of reserved sophistication as well as reduced the functionality of the garden. As it is, the two guiding qualities are delicately balanced in a garden that offers plenty of playing and living room.

Materials, Warmth, and Softness

METAL IS USUALLY PERCEIVED AS COLD AND HARD, BUT IT BECOMES WARM AND SOFT WHEN WROUGHT INTO PLEASING SHAPES. IT IS COOLER THAN PLANTS AND WOOD. IN HOT ENVIRONMENTS, METAL IS OFTEN HOT, IN COLD ENVIRONMENTS, VERY COLD—BUT IT IS USUALLY WARMER WHEN COATED OR PAINTED. WOOD IS USUALLY PERCEIVED AS WARM AND SOFT BUT CAN BE COOL AND SOFT, DEPENDING ON THE COLOR. NEW CEDAR IS WARM BUT, AS IT WEATHERS AND TURNS GRAY, BECOMES COOLER. TREATED WOOD RARELY LOOKS WARM. PLANTS CAN SOFTEN WOOD AND USUALLY MAKE IT COOLER, BUT NOT COLD. METAL POSTS AND CHAIN LINK ARE ALMOST ALWAYS COLD AND HARD. STONE CAN BE COOL AND HARD OR WARM AND SOFT, DEPENDING ON THE TYPE AND COLOR. GREY GRANITE, FOR EXAMPLE, IS BOTH HARD AND COLD WHILE ROSY OR TAN SANDSTONE IS WARM AND SOFT IN APPEARANCE. BRICK IS WARM AND CAN BE SOFT OR HARD, DEPENDING ON TYPE (USED BRICK IS SOFTER, NEW IS HARDER, FOR EXAMPLE) AND ON WHAT IT IS COMBINED WITH.

Design theme

The site itself lay in wait; it conveyed old-fashioned friendliness and was amenable to development. It lacked detail and sophistication. The owners possessed a quality of friendly sophistication and needed a space suited to their taste. *(top left and right)*

Organization of space

Two primary areas created by the patio-lawn juxtaposition are separated and joined by a simple arbor placed on a diagonal. The stepping-stone path to the right, the planting beds on both sides of the patio, and the raised bed in the rear add dimension. *(middle left)*

Structure

The lattice panels provide light but warm and sophisticated definition. *(middle right)*

Boundary structure

A perimeter fence made of a simple lattice without a cap maintains a light and informal feeling; the perforated fencing will fade into the planting. *(bottom left)*

Combination of materials

Paving stone, brick, grass, stone, wrought iron, foliage, and wood all contribute to rich textural combinations. *(bottom right)*

Proportion

The lawn balances with the paving; the planting beds balance with horizontal surfaces.

Summary of Details

Brick in the patio lightens the wall while harmonizing with it. The arch and fountain add rich dimensionality and tonal, architectural, and textural qualities. The lines of the patio add a touch of sophistication. The light arbor provides a gentle transition between the two primary areas. The plantings are combined with a view to textural and foliar color harmonies and contrasts.

Lessons from a Small Garden

Lyrical Garden

Designing with a Musical Motif

**Complexity
Level 8**

Garden size:
30 feet wide × 47 feet deep
(9.1 meters wide × 14.3 meters deep)

To discover the design theme of a small garden that lacks distinction, focus on its functions and the design inclinations of those who will enjoy it. In this garden, the lyrical sounds of water flowing and the musical motif tiles hint at a musical design, while small alcoves invite both play and reflection.

Perhaps unusual in that it needed to accommodate small gatherings of people, this small urban plot in a residential neighborhood otherwise possessed all the usual characteristics of a corner city property and posed all the usual challenges of transforming a static, rectilinear city-space into a graceful, inviting garden-space. As is not uncommon of many residential city lots, the site had been left undeveloped for a considerable period. It is shown here in a state of wreckage—the consequence of interior renovation. Whatever genius had once resided here no longer did, or at least it was well hidden. The design theme had to derive from the preferences of the inhabitants and the functions the garden would be asked to serve.

Above: The site before renovation.

A continuity of flowing lines through stone, brick, paving, and water creates a rhythmic effect, underscoring the musical motif of this garden.

Small Garden • Wisdom

Draw out the genius of a small urban garden with these techniques:

❋ Capitalize on the aural qualities of running water and fountains.

❋ Make the transitional walkway between street and garden a pleasant experience in itself.

❋ Pull complex designs together with materials that express the relationships among elements.

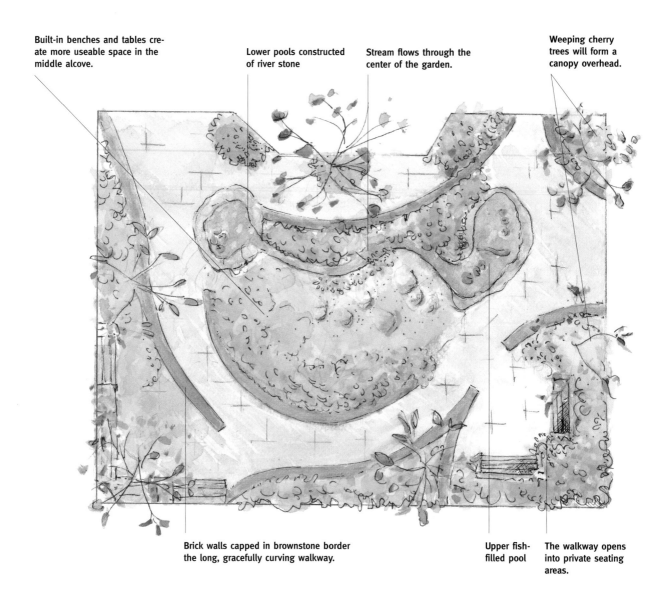

Built-in benches and tables create more useable space in the middle alcove.

Lower pools constructed of river stone

Stream flows through the center of the garden.

Weeping cherry trees will form a canopy overhead.

Brick walls capped in brownstone border the long, gracefully curving walkway.

Upper fish-filled pool

The walkway opens into private seating areas.

As the building's only usable outdoor area, the garden needed to accommodate a variety of purposes: to be inviting to the individual, to provide quiet places to sit, and to allow for several simultaneous small gatherings. It needed to have open areas for children and be able to withstand vigorous activity. It was also important that the garden be a visual asset to the neighborhood, as pleasing to see as in which to be. The owners asked only that the garden reflect and encourage an appreciation of music. This last became the guiding aesthetic influence through which all the functional requirements were satisfied.

Above: The design plan.

Left: A private seating area within the garden.

Make Sure Each Element Reinforces the Theme

Before examining the details of the finished garden, a look at the design theme is helpful. The intent was to create a garden that met specific needs and was lyrical, pleasurable, and visually appealing from all views. Elements needed within these parameters included a pleasant walkway, several seating areas, and an open space for children. In addition, the whole had to be graceful, attractive, and somehow reflective of the qualities of music. Each of the components of the finished garden emerged as integral to this design intent and exists as part of the whole.

The upper pool, audible at the point of entry, sounds the first musical note, inviting the visitor into the garden. From here, the garden begins to open; as the visitor walks through, it reveals details and intricacies—its medley of related components.

Create Walkways Worth Remembering

WHENEVER POSSIBLE, IT IS FAR BETTER TO DIRECT AN ENTRY WALK AWAY FROM THE BUILDING THROUGH A GARDEN AREA, AND TO GIVE IT A PLEASING LINE. PEOPLE TEND TO WANT A DIRECT, STRAIGHT WALK TO THE DOOR, SAYING THEY WILL ONLY CUT THROUGH TO THE MOST DIRECT ROUTE ANYWAY. BUT THIS IS NOT SO. ONCE A CURVING OR INDIRECT WALK IS IN PLACE, IT DOES BECOME THE ROUTE THAT IS USED—AND, IF IT IS MADE A PLEASANT EXPERIENCE, IT IS APPRECIATED. THE ENTRANCE TO A HOME IS GENERALLY THE FIRST IMPRESSION IT MAKES ON US, IT IS THE LAST IMPRESSION WE RECEIVE ON LEAVING, AND THESE IMPRESSIONS ARE OFTEN LASTING. IN MAKING GARDENS, RESIST FOCUSING EXCLUSIVELY ON FUNCTIONALITY TO THE DETRIMENT OF AESTHETICS.

The upper pool sounds the first musical note and issues the invitation into the garden.

Treat Garden Visitors to a Graceful Entryway

Before: The walkway (on the right of this image) sloped sharply down along the building to the front door. The balance of the site was a blank canvas waiting to be painted.

One of the primary flaws of the original layout was that the walkway ran along the building directly to the entrance. Every instance of coming and going was thus an entirely functional affair with no aesthetic or sensory considerations.

To create an entryway graceful to see and pleasurable to experience, and to prolong the transition from streetside to building, it is often best to locate the walk as far from the building as possible. When doing so, allow enough space for planting on both sides, and give the walk a long, sweeping curve. The idea is to slow people's usual hurried pace and focus their attention on the garden, bringing a touch of beauty to the transitional experience.

Bordered on both sides with brick walls opening into several alcoves, this walkway leisurely leads the visitor to and from the door while inviting detours into the private seating areas or the central area through which the stream flows. The wall is built of a manufactured used brick and capped in the same brownstone as that of the building. It brings a strong architectural element to the garden, helping the outdoor room balance with the building. The wall is also inset with brownstone and with musical motif tiles. The tiles carry on the design motif, and both tiles and stone help lighten what might otherwise have appeared an overly formal construction.

Interrupted Surfaces

A LARGE EXPANSE OF PLAIN, UNBROKEN SURFACE IS APPROPRIATE AS A BACKDROP TO MORE DECORATIVE ELEMENTS, AS INTERIOR WALLS ARE FOR FURNISHINGS, OR WHEN A FORMAL LOOK IS REQUIRED. ALONG THIS CURVING, GARDEN WALK, HOWEVER, SUCH A LOOK WOULD NOT HAVE SERVED THE DESIGN THEME. INSETTING STONES AND TILES IN A RANDOM PATTERN NOT ONLY ADDS CONSIDERABLE INTEREST TO THE WALL, IT PREVENTS IT FROM BEING TOO SERIOUS AND SOMBER A CONSTRUCTION.

Brick walls can be a formal, serious component of a garden. Here, they are lightened with insets of brownstone and tiles with musical motifs. This manufactured used brick was chosen to match the brick of the building; similarly, the brownstone coping harmonizes with its brownstone detailing.

Evoke Natural Beauty, Even in the City

The stream is an important feature of the garden. Made to look natural, it brings a bucolic touch to a city environment and helps both soften and enliven the space. The water falls from the upper pool and gently meanders down to two lower pools containing fish and water plants. Each water feature is meant to bring natural beauty and enjoyment to the area it occupies such that whether one is walking, standing, or seated, something is there to delight and please the senses. The stream and connected pools also serve to unite the garden along the long axis.

Exploit Materials to Unify Disparate Garden Elements

As one approaches the building entrance, a seating area opens to the right, retained by an arching wall that parallels the upper wall and runs along the stream. This wall is capped and inset with river stone rather than brownstone. Capping and insetting this wall with stone relates it to the other walls, while the river stone refers to the stream running just above it. In fact, some of the boulders that form the stream bed are also part of the capping, completing the connection.

A naturalistic stream is a pastoral element in an urban setting.

Contrast to the City

HARD LINES, HARSH SOUNDS, STARK BUILDINGS, MAN-MADE MATERIALS—THESE ELEMENTS CHARACTERIZE A CITY AND CAN GENERATE TENSION AND FATIGUE. THIS CERTAINLY IS A PRIMARY REASON WHY WE MAKE GARDENS—TO GIVE OURSELVES ANOTHER QUALITY OF EXPERIENCE. A GARDEN NEEDN'T BE DEFINED ONLY BY ITS PLANTS. SUCH ELEMENTS AS STREAMS AND POOLS AND THEIR NATURAL COUNTER-PARTS—FISH AND BIRDS—CAN PROVIDE TREMENDOUS PLEASURE. GARDENS OF ANY SIZE CAN CONTAIN THESE OTHER ELEMENTS, WHICH DO WONDERS TO NULLIFY THE HARSHNESS OF CITY LIFE AND PROVIDE A BALANCE TO THE CITY EXPERIENCE.

This wall relates to the other walls in that it is of brick, inset with tiles and stone, and capped with stone.

Top left: This upper pool serves as a wall that carries on the lines of the opposite walls. It is also the source of the stream flowing from it. The brick and brownstone gradually transitions into an all-river-stone construction.

Top right: The paving contributes to unification of place in that all the joint lines are exactly parallel or perpendicular to all the other joint lines.

This same attention to integrating the otherwise disparate components can also be seen in the upper and lower pools. Where the pools are a continuation of the wall and must follow its line, they are made of brick and brownstone—but because the upper pool is also the source of the stream and the bottom pool is the stream's termination, these pools transition from brick and brownstone into an all-river-stone construction. This blending of materials helps integrate the stream, brick wall, and pools into one dynamic unity.

Another unifying ingredient is the paving. The lines of the joints do not follow the line of the pathway or alter as they flow into the seating areas. Rather, they match up from end to end and side to side, with every line being exactly parallel or perpendicular to every other. A sub-level unification such as this can be unconsciously satisfying—similar to the effect of a unified pattern or color of wall-to-wall carpeting or the response to a lawn.

The seating areas themselves are meant to offer a range of possibilities. The lowest level contains a single bench backed by the warm wall of the building. It overlooks the lower pools and stream, providing a quiet place for solitary contemplation or quiet conversation.

Left: This middle seating area features built-in benches and compartments in which to place belongings.

Weave Private Nooks into the Fabric of the Garden

The middle alcove has built-in benches, beneath which are nooks for personal items, allowing more space for sitting or standing. There are also several small built-in tables for cups, plates, sandwiches, and such. This area is backed by a cedar and iron fence, partially enclosed with the brick, stone, and tile wall, and overlooks the length of the garden.

The upper seating area contains two benches looking toward the upper pool. Its view over the garden differs in angle from all others in the garden. The area is backed by foliage and flowers and is enclosed by the brick, stone, and tile walls. Although each area of the garden is unique and offers its own experiences, each is part of a whole, derives from that whole, and contributes to it.

The upper seating area over-looks the upper pool and the length of the garden.

The garden's color palette is expressed in hues of blue and purple, pink and rose.

Although the plantings have still to grow in, their general outlines may be discerned. The walk features weeping cherry trees on the left and an upright cherry and a weeping cherry on the right. These will, in time, form a canopy over the central portion of the walk, adding a delightful, romantic effect. The two red-leaved upright cherries at the property entrance stand like cheerful sentries. Other red-leaved plants appear throughout.

To soften extensive architectural elements, plant vines whenever possible along fences and on the building so that the garden is eventually enclosed entirely with foliage and flowers. Select a variety of groundcovers, grasses, and other appropriate shrubs and perennials, as along the length of this stream. As these plants grow, they will cover much of the visible stone, softening and naturalizing the area.

Consider the Quirks of Garden Users

All the seating areas are conducive to children's play, but the area along the stream, paved in river stone, attracts them most. Bear in mind that loose paving material may not be the best choice with children or dogs. Originally, loose, smooth river gravel was the paving material here, but the children were tempted to gather it into small handfuls and throw it about. The gravel was therefore removed and the river flats laid in a sand-cement mixture that keeps them in place. Children can watch the fish or play with their toys out of the way of others without threatening the plants.

The color palette for the planting is in ranges of blue to purple and pink to mauve to rose, with highlights of white. This was dictated by the intense hue of the brick walls, which harmonize with these colors but do not look well with others. Be sure to avoid yellow with this color of brick.

The intent for this garden was to create a varied but unified, lyrical environment—a pleasure to see and in which to be, inviting to the individual and accommodating small gatherings. All the elements—pools, stream, walls, seating areas, and planting beds—were designed to contribute to this effect. Although a small space, this garden contains numerous separate, yet well integrated areas, each offering its own experiential possibilities. It is this, above all, that generates the sense of expansiveness and multidimensionality.

This central area along the stream is the children's favorite play space.

Lessons from a Small Garden

Design theme
A musical motif expressed in a garden that serves the needs of individuals and small groups.

Organization of space
Complex. A central garden area with stream is encircled by two roughly parallel walls united by a stone and brick pool. A curving walk carves through the garden. Three seating areas branch off, forming a triangle. To both sides of the walls and walk, wherever possible, are planting beds, some raised, some at ground level. These many spaces within one space generate the sense of expansiveness.

Structure
Brick walls, benches, and boulders. These add mass to the garden and help it balance with the building.

Boundary structure
The building itself, a cedar fence, and iron picket fences. In time, these will be covered with foliage and blossoms.

Combination of materials
Brick with brownstone and terra-cotta tiles, brick with river stone, flagstone, wood, iron, river flats, and plants.

Proportion
Each area is spacious without taking too much from the whole. The walk is wide enough for two people to pass but could not be any wider. The height of the brick walls balances with the building but is not imposing. The stream and pools do not eat up too much of the usable space. The planting areas are large enough to balance the extensive structure in the garden; as they grow in, this will be achieved.

Summary of Details
Exhaustively applied in, for example, the brownstone-tinted grout of the capping stones, the placement of stones in the stream, the hand-carved tiles in the wall, planting choices, and stone pattern in the walks.

Bringing Out the Beauty in Narrow Garden Sites

Narrow sites can be among the most discouraging to encounter in the pursuit of garden making. Their linear quality seems to deny the possibility of creating depth, thereby implying the necessity of a garden in a straight line. On longer sites with specific access points, the task is still more difficult. They require passages through, if only to rake and tend, thereby requiring some sort of path. How do you make a path and garden and blend it for both convenience and beauty? Further, many sites are narrow because they are bounded on at least one side and often two by buildings. This tends to make them dark and somewhat stark and dreary. How to create attractive gardens in these settings is the focus of this chapter.

Narrow sites are generally not as narrow as they seem, if not compared to other gardens, and can be made to seem quite ample with proper placement of the right plants. Narrow planting beds can be made with the use of vines on trellises or vines that cling to a wall with a few upright plants at the base. Juxtaposed with plantings on the opposite side that sweep out toward the center of the plot generates a curve. This same pattern repeated further on, but with the narrow and fuller beds on the opposite sides, generates a curving motion through the garden that can then be accentuated by a path that follows that curve. This treatment greatly amplifies the available space. Further, horizontal layers of plants rising vertically from the base toward the sky add considerably to the garden's dimensionality.

Cinderella
Garden Plot

Using Plants as Structure in a Tiny Garden

Complexity Level 1

Garden size:
18 feet wide × 9 feet deep
(5.5 meters wide × 2.7 meters deep)

This forlorn orphan of a little plot was quietly anticipating transformation for years. Seen daily by the owners and passersby alike, it needed care, beautifying, a touch of elegance—it needed to be dressed up and turned out properly. Though not a garden that would be used, it certainly was full of latent potential for loveliness.

This notion of bringing a little glamour and sophistication to this narrow piece of land, of dressing up the garden and its lone Japanese Maple, became the concept around which the design evolved.

Graceful flowing motion—somehow introduced—would relieve the static quality of the tiny rectangular plot. The harsh walls and fence could be clothed in vines. The space would revel in an abundance of attractive, well-placed shrubs, and the maple would show to advantage with an underplanting of appropriate shrubs and perennials.

Above: An orphaned plot quietly longing for attention.

Juxtaposed plant masses serve as structural elements within a small garden.

Small Garden ——•—— Wisdom	**Be a benefactor to some abandoned bit of garden:**
	❋ Add to the world's beauty by rejuvenating a neglected, lonely garden plot. ❋ Remember that even tiny, narrow beds can grow lush with foliage and flowers. ❋ Skirt a mature tree with a mound of plants, like the plinth of a column.

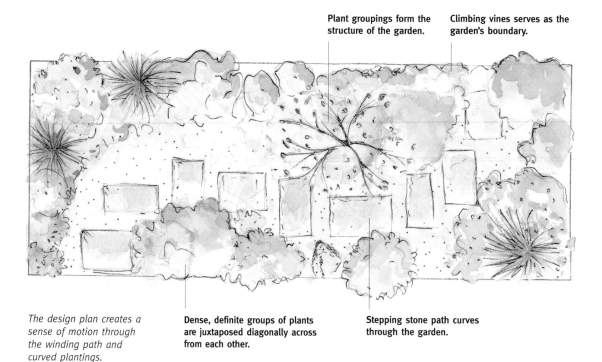

Plant groupings form the structure of the garden.

Climbing vines serves as the garden's boundary.

The design plan creates a sense of motion through the winding path and curved plantings.

Dense, definite groups of plants are juxtaposed diagonally across from each other.

Stepping stone path curves through the garden.

A Winding Path

To achieve a sense of motion, planting beds were designed to hug the side while, opposite from them, plants sweep out toward the center. This pattern was repeated in reverse along the long axis. A stepping-stone path was laid such that it winds from the outside of one end of the garden through the middle to the inside of the other end. Intended both for visual effect and practical use, it sweeps through the garden in a gentle curve, inviting the eye to follow and, practically, permitting access for tending the plants.

Garden Plantings

In a garden such as this—that, because of its dimensional limitations, permits little use of structure—plants take on special significance. Plants delineate a small space by serving as structure within the garden. At the same time, they must generate interest and provide variety while still allowing a sense of place or unity.

To achieve this, mass plants in dense, defined groups placed in juxtaposition to one another, and separate them by smaller plants or by space. Notice the rose and hydrangea grouping, offset diagonally across the path from the hydrangea and miscanthus planting. These masses create structural form within the garden as well as add balance and harmony.

A stepping-stone path gracefully arches through the garden.

Such groupings also make possible exciting foliar and flower contrasts and pleasing harmonies. The delicate leaves and flowers of the rose, for example, contrast wonderfully with those of the hydrangea, while the flower colors harmonize. Similarly, the lavender and hydrangea both harmonize and contrast, as do the lavender and the hosta, the hosta and the miscanthus, and the miscanthus and the hydrangea. These complex relationships, reaching through the garden, convey richness and motion by virtue of their visual interactions.

Utilize the Relativity of Size

PARTICULARLY WHEN WORKING IN VERY CRAMPED SITES, REMEMBER THAT PERCEPTIONS OF SIZE ARE RELATIVE. A PLANTING BED THAT WOULD SEEM RIDICULOUSLY SMALL ON A LARGER SITE MAY BE SUITABLE WHERE THE ENTIRE GARDEN IS SPATIALLY LIMITED. THIS IS WHY DIMINUTIVE JAPANESE GARDENS OR TINY ROCK GARDENS WORK. EVERY COMPONENT OF THE GARDEN IS SEEN IN RELATION TO EVERY OTHER, AND, SO LONG AS RULES OF PROPORTION ARE NOT VIOLATED, THE ENTIRE CREATION CAN SEEM AMPLE AND COMPLETE. ON NARROW SITES, A PLANTING BED ONLY 1 FOOT (30 CM), OR SO, DEEP CAN BE PERFECTLY APPROPRIATE—UTILIZING THE SPACE THIS WAY WILL ALLOW THE CREATION OF A COMPLETE GARDEN THAT DOES NOT SEEM SMALL.

Top: Massed groupings create structure in the garden.

Above: Foliar and flower contrasts and harmonies add richness and interest to the garden.

Exploit the Textural and Formal Qualities of Plants to Add Dimension

To soften fences and walls, select climbing vines such as climbing hydrangea, wisteria, and clematis, as shown here. The texture and beauty of such plants become the garden's boundaries. The Japanese maple has a skirt of skimmia japonica, chosen for its neat habit, its evergreen quality, and its bright, ornamental berries. This forms a rounded mass at the base of the maple, which balances with the two hydrangea plantings on either side of it.

A Well-Turned-Out Garden

The repetition of textures and forms throughout the garden—the hydrangeas, hostas, grasses, and daylilies, for instance—gives the garden unity through diversity, while the bright foliage and blossoms of perennials and annuals add highlights. Perfume is provided by lavender, wisteria, and rose, capturing the attention of passersby who now stop to admire this once neglected and now well-dressed garden plot.

Above: These Skimmia japonica form an elegant skirt for the Japanese Maple.

Right: From an orphaned plot to an elegant garden.

Lessons from a Small Garden

Design theme
Dressing up and beautifying an orphaned site. *(top left)*

Organization of space
Created primarily through plant groupings juxtaposed along the curvy axis of the garden path. *(top right)*

Structure
Almost none, except the stepping-stone pathway and the existing maple tree. *(top left and right)*

Boundary structure
The existing walls and fences.

Combination of materials
Plant groupings with the backdrop of fences and wall. *(bottom left)*

Proportion
The lawn balances with the paving; the planting beds balance with horizontal surfaces. *(bottom right)*

Summary of Details
The strongly contrasting and harmonizing foliage and flowers throughout the garden.

Welcoming Entry Garden Court

Providing Elegance with Brick Walls and Planters

Complexity Level 2

Garden size:
16 feet wide × 7 feet deep
(4.9 meters wide × 2.1 meters deep)

Adding elegant raised beds and planters and organizing unattractive necessities out of the way helped transform this entranceway into a stunning garden court.

This space, the front of an otherwise elegant co-op, was, of necessity, utilitarian—but unnecessarily harsh and unattractive. Trash receptacles needed to be stored in the vicinity, but the area's only other use was as a waiting room. Apart from a couple of disintegrating half-barrels planted in forlorn junipers, nothing had been done to render the space a little less offensive, a little more amenable for visitors and residents alike. Indeed, the owners wondered if anything could be done. The concrete flooring, the exposed trash receptacles, the barren harshness of it all—could these shortcomings be overcome?

Above: Could this barren place become a garden?

OFTEN, IN URBAN SETTINGS, IT IS NOT POSSIBLE TO REMOVE CERTAIN REALITIES—VIEWS OF BUILDINGS AND TELEPHONE WIRES, CITY SOUNDS, AND SO ON. BUT IT IS POSSIBLE TO MASK THEM SUFFICIENTLY, OR TO CREATE AN OPPOSING REALITY—AN ABUNDANTLY PLANTED, WELL DESIGNED GARDEN FILLS OUR SENSES WITH ANOTHER, HIGHLY PLEASING REALITY. HERE, THIS GRACEFULLY CURVING BRICK WALL DOES NOT COMPLETELY HIDE THE UNWANTED VIEWS, BUT EFFECTIVELY SEPARATES US FROM THEM. IN CONJUNCTION WITH THE OTHER BRICK PLANTERS AND THEIR PLANTS, THE NEGATIVE ELEMENTS ARE RENDERED LARGELY BENIGN.

After: An elegant entry court to an urban residence.

Small Garden
● Wisdom

Grace an entranceway with raised beds and planters, to the delight of all:

❋ Use plants of varying heights to flood the garden with abundance and charm.

❋ Partially obscure objects of necessity so they do not confront people going in and out.

❋ Pave over unattractive concrete to visually soften the surface and make it less rigid.

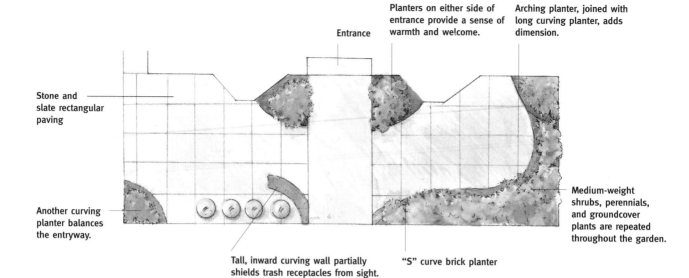

Planters on either side of entrance provide a sense of warmth and welcome.

Arching planter, joined with long curving planter, adds dimension.

Entrance

Stone and slate rectangular paving

Medium-weight shrubs, perennials, and groundcover plants are repeated throughout the garden.

Another curving planter balances the entryway.

Tall, inward curving wall partially shields trash receptacles from sight.

"S" curve brick planter

Make Virtues of a Site's Limitations

Above: The design plan.

The flaws of the site and the sophistication exhibited by the owners led to the solutions. Easy access to the receptacles needed to be maintained, but they could be organized all to one side and partially shielded from exposure. The rest of the area could contain raised beds of a distinguished construction and softening design. The planters themselves, if well-designed and built, would lend a degree of elegance to the structure of the site and would allow for an abundance of shrubs, perennials, and a small tree or two. This would soften the entire scene and transform this entry space into an entry garden court. Likewise, planters on either side of the door would bring an elegance to the entrance itself and endow the property with a polished look.

A tall, inward-curving wall on the left provides the barrier for the receptacles—still easily accessed and partially visible, but substantially separated and essentially removed from the experience of the arrival and departure.

The other side of the entryway, which needed to serve only as a waiting area, is now the primary garden-court. A brick planter designed in an S-shape extends up the side of the long axis and is intersected by an arching planter, itself intercepted by another arching planter in the diagonal corner. The joining of these separate planting spaces adds dimensionality to the design. Two more planters embrace the entrance. They provide a warm, welcoming element and a definite sense of entrance. Another curving planter occupies the other extreme end of the site, balancing the whole.

Top two: A series of connected planters brings sophistication and grace to the site, helping create a garden court.

As the before and after images indicate, these entrance planters offer a warm welcome and provide a definite sense of entrance previously absent.

The original paving was all concrete—highly functional but rarely aesthetically appealing. It was paved over with stone and slate in mixed shades of gray, green, and brown, which together harmonize with the cream color of the building. Laid in a random rectangular pattern, the new paving gives a finished look to the garden court.

Load Planters for Year-Round Variety and Interest

The final transformation comes through the planting scheme. The challenge in small, tight sites such as this is to provide structure, variety, and seasonal interest without using too many different species. In the long, S-curved planter, a weeping cherry on the far end balances with a kousa dogwood at the other and an upright juniper in the diagonal corner. Dwarf rhododendron and dwarf weeping hemlock scattered about give winter interest and intermediate-level structure. Woven among these medium-height shrubs are smaller perennials, and beneath these are groundcover plants, some of which will spill over the walls as they grow. Repeated throughout the garden, these help unify the planting scheme. In the entrance planters, the branching of the dwarf Japanese maples gives winter interest, while the foliage is delightful from spring through fall. Ferns beneath repeat the light, airy look.

Though fairly bleak and unpromising at the outset, this co-op entry is now the star front garden of the neighborhood and a delight to its owners—showing how a little planning, a few simple lines on paper, can lead to a pleasant garden court.

Lessons from a Small Garden

Design theme
Invoke the site's opposite attributes and bring them in keeping with the structure. Gracefully obscure utilitarian necessities.

Organization of space
A single, narrow rectangle was portioned into a central waiting area with planters on all sides.

Structure
The raised brick planters give good, balanced structure to the garden and harmonize with the structure of the building.

Boundary structure
The building on one side, iron picket fence on the other.

Combination of materials
Brick, slate, iron, and plants.

Proportion
The planters could not be larger without impinging on the central gathering area or higher without being out of scale with the width of the area.

Summary of Details
In the line of the planters and the combinations of plants.

Transformed Garden Deck

Creating Interest with Decking, Lattice, and Ornament

Complexity Level 4

Garden size:
51 feet wide × 9 feet deep
(15.5 meters wide × 2.7 meters deep)

Interconnected decks with an abundance of plants in containers enliven a dark and narrow plot. Enhance the positive attributes of a garden space—although they may be hard to find—and remove or mask unwanted features.

This project posed a variety of challenges. Like many urban backyards, it was exceedingly narrow, dark, and uninviting. To be of value, the space would need to be made accessible, usable, and attractive. The treatment and design of this garden is applicable to any long, narrow property and is particularly relevant to rooftop gardens, which frequently possess the same restrictive qualities—that is, narrowness and the impossibility of in-ground planting, in this case because of below-grade utilities and an abundance of concrete.

Above: Before. An unpromising site for a garden.

A series of interconnected decks with four elevation changes reduces the sense of narrowness. A variety of container plantings adds dimensionality.

Small Garden
Wisdom

Step up to the challenge of long, narrow garden plots with these approaches:

* Face the limitations of a garden space squarely to enable solutions to come to mind.
* Learn to love container gardening when in-ground planting is unsuitable.
* Be inventive in obscuring necessary evils such as pipes and utility meters.

A variety of potted plants lend visual interest.

Bench

Lattice panels hide unsightly
wires and pipes.

Wall fountain

Arbor

Single steps connect the
four deck areas.

Reenvision a Difficult Space as Lovely

Some sites seem so dispossessed of any quality reminiscent of a garden as to appear absolutely incapable of becoming one. Rarely is this actually true. Generally, the possibilities for alteration are considerable. Begin by mentally noting the undesirable elements and conceiving of ways to alter, remove, or mask them.

Transforming this space into a garden both enjoyable to inhabit and attractive to see required a complete reenvisioning of the space. It was cluttered with wires and utilities and was dark and gloomy, confining, completely static, and generally unlovely (on this site, just about everything was undesirable).

The walls were mostly cinderblock or painted brick and were marred with wires, pipes, and utilities, all of which had to stay. The solution was to build lattice panels over them, with openings as needed to permit access to the utilities. The ground surface also contained unattractive components that had to stay but to which access was only rarely needed. Decking and built-in movable modules proved the solution to this. The air conditioning units were movable and, thus, could be relocated.

Equally important as recognizing the undesirable elements is to identify positive attributes that can be enhanced; there nearly always are some. Here, the length of the property meant that variations could be incorporated in a variety of ways. Some areas, for example, could contain groupings of small ornamental pots while in other areas larger containers, trellises, or even a pergola could be employed. The other desirable attribute—the old burgundy brick wall—could be framed out and embellished. When viewing a site that seems hopeless, imagine it in the opposite condition; this leads to solutions that can engender a garden.

It is Better to Plant One Plant Than to Curse the Bareness

THERE IS OFTEN A TENDENCY ON REALLY DISCOURAGING SITES TO THROW UP ONE'S HANDS IN DEFEAT, BUT THIS IS ALMOST NEVER NECESSARY. TAKE ONE SINGLE STEP—CLEAR AWAY SOME DEBRIS OR PLANT A PLANT, OR LAY UP A NARROW PIECE OF LATTICE AND PLACE A PLANTED POT AT THE BASE. YOU WILL REALIZE INSTANTLY THAT THE PLACE CAN BE IMPROVED, AND THIS WILL INEVITABLY LEAD TO TAKING ANOTHER STEP, AND ANOTHER, AND BEFORE LONG, YOU HAVE A GARDEN WHERE ONCE THERE WAS A WASTELAND.

Plant in Containers to Glorious Effect

As the design plan shows, this garden was conceived as a series of decks separated by an elevation change of only a single step. Seating areas with tables occupy both ends. Benches are set against the wall, roughly in the middle. The bleakness of the site evoked the desire for an abundance of plants, which, because of the unsuitable nature of the terrain, had to be planted in containers.

One of the primary intents of the owner was to have a variety of planted containers on display, so a greater quantity and variety of pots and planters was used than might otherwise have been chosen. For example, had the intent been to use the deck garden for entertainment, more space would have been left for standing and sitting. Nevertheless, variety in the size and shape of containers can contribute substantially to the effect of a container garden. An eclectic combination of planted containers is part of this garden's charm.

Vary Planters as Well As Your Plants—and Their Placement, Too

USE MANY SIZES, SHAPES, AND MATERIALS FOR CONTAINERS ON DECKS, ROOFTOP GARDENS, PATIOS, AND OTHER SITES REQUIRING CONTAINER PLANTING. ALTHOUGH IT IS CERTAINLY POSSIBLE TO BE TOO ECLECTIC (THE PRESENT PROJECT IS, PERHAPS, A CASE IN POINT), A VARIETY OF CONTAINERS NOT ONLY CREATES THE GREATEST VISUAL APPEAL BUT ALSO SUITS A VARIETY OF PLANTS. IT IS OFTEN BEST TO USE TWO OR MORE PLANTS IN LARGER CONTAINERS, PERHAPS AN UPRIGHT SPECIMEN WITH TRAILING PLANTS BENEATH IT. THE QUALITY OF FLOWING MOTION CAN BE ACHIEVED EVEN ON A STRAIGHT, NARROW DECK BY PLACING CONTAINERS OF DIFFERENT SIZES AND SHAPES ON BOTH SIDES OF THE WALKWAY, THEREBY DIRECTING THE FLOW OF TRAFFIC IN A MORE UNDULATING LINE.

It's hard to believe this is the same space, now that it's been transformed.

Architectural ornament relieves the monotony of barren walls and permits the softening effect of plants. Notice the rich, foliar contrasts and pleasing harmonies.

Liberate the Site with Ornament and Movement

The barren block and painted brick walls called out for ornamentation. This was provided in the form of trellises in architectural forms. In addition to breaking up the stark surfaces with their own pleasing designs, the trellises permit vines to clamber about, softening the otherwise harsh surfaces. The next step in the plan is to install wall fountains.

The deck could have been laid all on one elevation, but creating a single step from one major area to another enhances the sense of moving through a multidimensional space. It also reduces the sense of confinement the narrowness of the space projects. Stepping up onto or down into another level has the effect of entering another room, and this compartmentalizing the long axis reduces the sense of narrowness. The variety of plants, which yields dynamic contrasts and pleasing harmonies, also stimulates the eye and contributes to the dimensionality of this once seemingly hopeless site.

The finished garden. Compare this to the before image.

Design theme

This site was so lacking in garden qualities, it evoked its opposite—a jungle of bright foliage and flowers planted, at the owner's request, in a great variety of planters and pots. The strengths of the site—its length and some attractive features—were put to use and made enjoyable. *(top left)*

Organization of space

The sense of restriction resulting from the site's narrowness was diminished by segmenting the decking into four elevation changes, creating connected, flow-through rooms. *(top left)*

Structure

Considerable structure already existed in the walls, and the deck, a necessity, added more structure. This is why the abundance of planting works without being overwhelming. *(bottom left and right)*

Boundary structure

Walls, walls everywhere. *(top right)*

Combination of materials

Plants, wood, terra cotta, and glazed ceramic. *(top left)*

Proportion

The height of the planted containers lowers the perceived height of the walls.

Summary of Details

The variety of planters, pots, and foliage, primarily, plus other garden ornaments.

Lessons from a Small Garden

Graceful Garden Walk

Adding Harmony and Motion with Foliage and Flower

Complexity Level 2

Garden size:
45 feet wide × 8 feet deep
(13.7 meters wide × 2.4 meters deep)

Typical of many residential apartment buildings and co-op properties, this garden is bordered on one side by the building and on the other by a fence. Had it not needed to function as an access route, creating a garden here would have been easy, but a wide path was, indeed, mandated. Making it into both a graceful walkway and an attractive garden was the challenge.

Above: The walk during construction. The sense of curvy motion will be accentuated by planting the available spaces created by staggering the stones.

A graceful garden walk, dramatically planted.

Nature and the Curving Line

TRY TO PLAN A CURVED PATH-WAY WHENEVER POSSIBLE. IT HAS OFTEN BEEN POINTED OUT THAT THERE ARE NO STRAIGHT LINES IN NATURE. ANYONE WHO HAS WALKED IN THE WOODS ALSO KNOWS THAT THE SAME IS TRUE OF THE PATH-WAYS ANIMALS MAKE IN THEIR DAILY RAMBLINGS. PEOPLE ARE AS MUCH A PART OF NATURE AS DEER AND, THOUGH A STRAIGHT WALK MAY BE PRAC-TICAL AND LESS EXPENSIVE IN MANY APPLICATIONS, IT IS RARELY AS SATISFYING TO SEE AND TO WALK AS A PATH THAT GENTLY SWAYS AS IT LEADS TO ITS DESTINATION.

Small Garden ● Wisdom	**Make visual music of a garden walkway using these ideas:**
	❀ Avoid overly straight walks, which preclude imaginative planting. ❀ Consider negotiating elevation changes in a walkway with steps rather than a slope. ❀ Take advantage of the infinite variety in plants—the color and shape of leaves, height, and so on.

Top: Low steps, evenly spaced
up the walk, convey a sense
of lift. Seen from the other
end, the view is of a pleasant,
gradual descent.

The tendency on such a site is to run the walkway right up the middle of the space and try to plant the sides. The result is, generally, a static, graceless walk and insipid planting beds of constrictive narrowness. Here, the walk was staggered for two reasons: one, to take greatest advantage of the alcoves of the building—which yielded more planting space; and two, to generate curve and motion in the walk and variation in the beds. As the walk shifts from side to side, its width expands from side to side as well, accentuating the sense of motion.

Because of the 2-foot (.6 m) elevation change from one end to the other, four 6-inch (15 cm) steps were built into the walk. Though not entirely necessary, this allowed for a level walk—more visually appealing and easier to use than a sloped one. Six inches (15 cm) is an appropriate outdoor rise of step and, as all the steps are the same height, they are comfortable to use. These slight elevation changes, evenly spaced up the walk, give a visual sense of lift from one end and a pleasant sense of easy descent when seen from the other.

The walkway comfortably falls
in flat plains from the back to
the front.

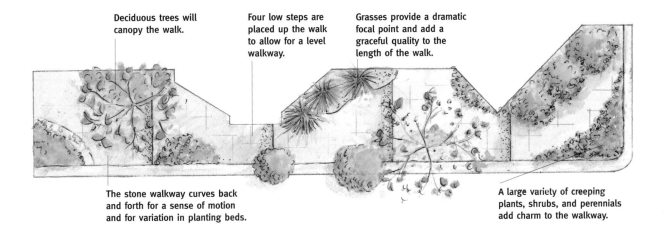

Deciduous trees will canopy the walk.

Four low steps are placed up the walk to allow for a level walkway.

Grasses provide a dramatic focal point and add a graceful quality to the length of the walk.

The stone walkway curves back and forth for a sense of motion and for variation in planting beds.

A large variety of creeping plants, shrubs, and perennials add charm to the walkway.

Go for Broke When Grouping Plants

Plant choice was key to the success of this garden walk. Such spaces are usually planted in ordinary groupings of rhododendron, azalea, arbor vitae, and such. Although this does give flowers during the spring and greenery through the year, it is never particularly attractive. This garden has a few evergreen plants spaced randomly throughout, but it supports an unusual variety of deciduous shrubs and perennials, creating effects not possible with the usual foundation plants. It is these, in conjunction with the pleasing path, that give this garden walk its peculiar charm.

Notice in particular the detailed harmonies and contrasts within individual groupings. The variegated berberis has similar branching, leaf size, shape, and markings to the variegated euonymus, but contrasting leaf color; at the same time, it has contrasting leaf size to the prunus cistena but harmonizes with it in leaf color. In that grouping, the variegated Iris harmonizes in color with the euonymus and in form to both the euonymus and the berberis while contrasting in leaf color with the berberis and prunus cistena. The grasses harmonize with the upright quality of the berberis, euonymus, and iris while contrasting with the round leaf of the prunus. Here is a complexity of relationships between and among the members of a grouping. This is what stimulates the eye and excites the appreciation.

Simultaneous harmonies and contrasts in form, leaf shape, and color among several genera create exciting groupings.

Plan for Dramatic Focal Points

The grasses sound an important chord in this composition. Repeated throughout the walkway beds and to both sides, they provide dramatic focal points along the entire length, they make wonderful harmonies with similarly leaved plants, such as Daylily and Iris, and they provide beautiful counterpoint to rounder-leaved plants and creeping plants, such as Juniper. Most important, they add a feminine, graceful quality as they weep and sweep over the walk. They catch the light and sway in the breeze beautifully, bringing yet more motion and rhythm to the entire composition.

Finally, contributing to the almost musical quality of this garden walk, rhythm is created by the great variations in plant genus. Deciduous trees will canopy over the walk to about 15 feet, a few narrow conifers will reach considerably higher than that, and vines grow on both the fence and against the building. Variety is the name of the game for creeping plants, midrange shrubs, and a wealth of perennials.

All these factors—the graceful curve of the walk, the elevation changes, the rich harmonies and contrasts of foliage and flowers, and the rhythmic undulations of plant height—create a pleasing garden walk within a narrow confine.

The Versatility of Foliage

NEVER UNDERESTIMATE THE IMPORTANCE AND IMPACT OF FOLIAGE. AS LOVELY AS BLOSSOMS ARE, THEY ARE OFTEN OVEREMPHASIZED TO THE POINT WHERE THE GARDEN'S OVERALL BEAUTY SUFFERS. AN INDIVIDUAL PLANT'S FLOWERS LAST BUT A SHORT WHILE, SO PLANTS MUST OFTEN BE COMBINED IN GROUPINGS THAT DO NOT LOOK GOOD TOGETHER IN ORDER TO CREATE A SUCCESSION OF BLOOMS—WHEN BLOOM IS THE CHIEF CONCERN. FOLIAGE, HOW-EVER, ENDURES FROM SPRING THROUGH FALL, AND THE DELIGHTFUL COMBINATIONS THAT CAN BE MADE WITH IT ARE VIRTUALLY ENDLESS.

Above: Ornamental grasses bring a light, airy touch to the walk.

Lessons from a Small Garden

Design theme
Harmonious motion through a narrow channel. *(top left, bottom left and right)*

Organization of space
Walkway and planting were divided along a curving axis roughly up the middle of the available area while swinging both right and left. *(top and bottom left)*

Structure
The stone of the walkway.

Boundary structure
The building on one side, the iron fence on the other.

Combination of materials
Stone and plants, plants and brick building, and plants and iron fence. *(top right)*

Proportion
It was important that the walk be wide enough to invite use and that the planting areas be balanced on both sides of the walkway. *(bottom left)*

Summary of Details
The line of the walk and, especially, the planting combinations.

Creating the Elements of Mystery and Discovery

A primary flaw of many small gardens is that they are completely apprehended in a single glance. One step out the door and there it is, a single space completely lacking in mystery, surprise, and adventure. In previous chapters, we discussed dividing and terracing to add dimensionality and interest to a small garden while making it feel more expansive. Here are four gardens in which the quality of mystery and the experience of discovery are used to enhance charm and dimensionality.

The principle is simple. When one enters a garden space that appears to extend into some unseen area, a slight excitement is generated. One wants to pursue the mystery. Though the distance between the entry point and the half-hidden garden is only a few short steps, that little separation does wonders by adding the delightful element of surprise. As one passes the final barrier or rounds the corner and steps into the mysterious beyond, he or she experiences a moment of sudden discovery and, once in the garden proper, appreciates the separation and seclusion that results from its concealment.

Beyond the element of discovery, astonishment and a sense of the mysterious can be generated through an unconventional motif and by the skillful use of materials, as demonstrated in the last example in this chapter.

Garden Oasis in an Urban Setting

Building a Sense of Discovery with Curves and Screening

Complexity Level 2

Garden size:
22 feet wide × 30 feet deep
(6.7 meters wide × 9.1 meters deep)

Create a private garden away from tall buildings and undesirable views by screening the patio and garden perimeter with an abundance of plants and trees. Avoid a direct path to the patio—an indirect walkway builds a sense of discovery as it meanders along, fetching up at the patio. A small pond on the way adds to the enjoyment of the garden.

Initially, this urban garden consisted of a walkway around the perimeter and planting in the middle. It worked well as a specimen garden, but it failed as a landscape. Everything was apparent; there were no outdoor living areas and, from within the garden, one was entirely visible from neighboring buildings that were likewise fully in view. The garden seemed smaller than its actual 22 feet by 30 feet (6.7 meters by 9.1 meters) and was not a pleasant place to be.

Above: An uninspired and exposed space waiting to become a private oasis.

Privacy is achieved in an urban setting by surrounding the patio with leafy trees and shrubs that screen out unwanted views.

<table>
<tr><td rowspan="2">Small Garden
——•——
Wisdom</td><td>**When seeking seclusion in the midst of urban exposure, try these approaches:**</td></tr>
<tr><td>❋ Plant trees to screen a central space from both house and surrounding buildings.
❋ Design meandering pathways to engender an element of surprise and discovery.
❋ Avoid the straight edges that tend to make urban gardens rigid in feel.</td></tr>
</table>

Dedicate Space to Pathways for a Sense of Discovery

CITY GARDENS HAVE NO ROOM TO WASTE. MOST OF THE AVAILABLE AREA NEEDS TO BE DEDICATED TO OUTDOOR LIVING AND TO PLANTING. PATHS, HOWEVER, THOUGH PERHAPS NOT AS IMPORTANT AS DESTINATIONS, ARE A DESIGN ELEMENT NOT TO BE DISCOUNTED—ESPECIALLY IN A GARDEN, WHICH IS INTENDED TO EVOKE PLEASURABLE RESPONSES. THOUGH A FEW FEET OF POTENTIAL PLANTING AREA ARE LOST, WINDING THE WALK AROUND AND ONLY GRADUALLY ACHIEVING THE DESTINATIONS BEYOND HEIGHTENS THE SENSE OF DISCOVERY AS EACH STEP BRINGS MORE DELIGHTFUL ELEMENTS TO THE EXPERIENCE. FINALLY, AT THE END OF THE PATH, ONE HAS A PALPABLE SENSE OF ARRIVAL AND DISCOVERY.

Above: A water garden and planting bed allow glimpses of the garden beyond while directing the visitor around and through overhanging foliage. Only gradually is the garden revealed.

Opposite: Framed views into neighboring trees make them part of this garden.

What this garden desperately needed was concealment. It was exposed to the world, and that exposure had a stifling effect. It wanted privacy, secrecy, and a little surprise. To achieve that effect here several considerable changes were required.

In order to gain outdoor living areas and to help create privacy, the existing plan needed to be reversed. The planting was relocated to the outside and the paving moved to the interior. This allows for sufficient patio space, screened by planting buffers. To completely separate the patio from the house, the path from the door leads around to the right between planting beds, rather than going directly to the living areas beyond. This also made space for a planting screen directly between the home and the patio.

To enhance the sense of discovery and to add to the enjoyment of the garden as a whole, a small pond was built just beyond the first planting area, between the patio and the walkway. Stepping from the door onto the garden walk, one hears the sounds of water gurgling over stones and catches a glimpse of the pond and areas beyond. Following the path, parting the branches of Dogwood and Crape Myrtle, one suddenly comes upon the open garden, a private sanctuary. On the patio, the visitor is enveloped in a luxuriance of plantings and provided with a variety of views and outdoor living possibilities, including a stone barbecue. The pond now is fully visible, lapping against the patio edge, while a table seating eight invites garden dining. The trees and shrubs screen buildings while framing views into neighboring trees that become part of the garden experience, expanding it beyond its boundaries.

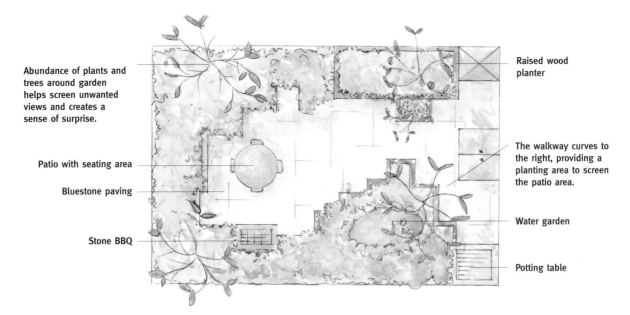

Abundance of plants and trees around garden helps screen unwanted views and creates a sense of surprise.

Patio with seating area

Bluestone paving

Stone BBQ

Raised wood planter

The walkway curves to the right, providing a planting area to screen the patio area.

Water garden

Potting table

To contribute to the quality of softness this garden was intended to possess, the walk and patio were given an irregular edge. Breaking up the lines this way permits edging and sprawling plants to form the patio's soft, irregular border, eliminating the rectilinear effect so typical of urban gardens and rounding the space to a natural softness.

Because of these elements—the abundant perennials, trees, and shrubs, the screening of unwanted and the capturing of desirable views, the gradual way by which the garden is discovered, and the enjoyment of privacy within a garden world—nearly everyone who comes here describes it as an oasis, which is why they look forward to returning.

Lessons from a Small Garden

Design theme
Modest pleasure in a private oasis.

Organization of space
A patio separated from the house and surrounded by plantings and a water garden.

Structure
The stone barbecue, one raised bed, and a few terra-cotta planters, plus candle stands placed about the garden.

Boundary structure
Lattice-topped fences on three sides, the building on the fourth.

Combination of materials
Stone, plants, and water.

Proportion
The patio is just large enough to accommodate small parties without being so large as to take away from the planting areas. The water garden is likewise designed to fill a niche without encroaching on the living areas.

Summary of Details
Almost exclusively in the planting scheme, which is quite varied.

Urban Mediterranean Garden

Revealing the Garden in Glimpses

Complexity Level 3

Garden size:
17 feet wide × 16 feet deep
(5.2 meters wide × 4.9 meters deep)

The owners of this garden enjoy the simple pleasures of life as well as the more rarified. Their desire was for a place pleasant to be, with charm, harmony, and privacy. Natural gardeners and devoted plant lovers, they hoped to sun in the chaise by day and relax in the evening, discussing their day over drinks amid an abundance of flora.

The site seemed small and was closely encroached upon by neighboring buildings. It was, as is so often the case in urban environments, static, it lacked charm, and was replete with disagreeable views. The degree to which it did not suit the owners was glaring. Yet these negative attributes were not inherent in the site. There was plenty of room to make a garden more to the owners' tastes. The space simply had never been relieved of the unimaginative layout so characteristic of city gardens. Merely perceiving this, and under-standing it, led to the garden's design.

Above: Before its makeover, this garden plat had a typical urban layout—static, unin-spired, and restrictive.

A planting screen placed near the entry partially masks the patio area beyond.

Small Garden
●
Wisdom

Add vibrancy and a sense of discovery to a static garden:

❀ Bring plantings to the entryway, and place a screening bed further into the garden.

❀ Incorporate brightly colored tiles into brick raised beds.

❀ Use bamboo's leafy abundance to screen views and create interest.

Plan for Pets in the Garden

Flowing motion, soft curves, and lush abundance were needed in order to create the relaxed, informal, yet quietly rich environment that seemed desirable. The space needed to be delineated in such a way as to provide adequate and graceful living room while allowing ample planting. Unpleasant views needed to be screened and the living area carved out of the available space. Curved beds would contribute to the desired softness, a focal point would add interest, and a sense of mystery or surprise would help expand the experience of the garden. Privacy was essential. Two small dogs were part of the family and had to be provided for. In short, a complete transformation was necessary.

Raised beds serve several purposes in this garden. They provide good planting areas above the growth-retardant roots of a large tree that once grew there, they protect the plants from the dogs, and they provide auxiliary seating during parties without cluttering the available space with furniture. From a purely design perspective, they add a graceful strength previously lacking in the garden.

In this case, brick was chosen for building the raised beds. It goes well with the desired paving of irregular pieces of fieldstone, is inexpensive, and lends itself to curves. The notion of colored tiles incorporated into the walls arose from the contagiously bright and cheerful quality of the owners; these now ornament the walls throughout. All in the blue and blue-green range, the tiles harmonize with the garden and help bring a bit of the garden's lightness and life to its vertical structures and instill the garden with a Mediterranean quality.

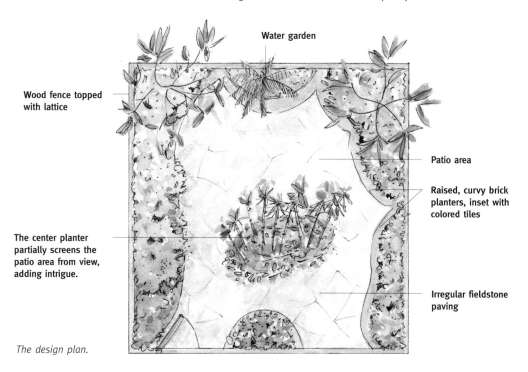

Water garden

Wood fence topped with lattice

Patio area

Raised, curvy brick planters, inset with colored tiles

The center planter partially screens the patio area from view, adding intrigue.

Irregular fieldstone paving

The design plan.

Bring the Garden Up to Its Entry Point

Consider Ornament

ORNAMENT CAN BE AN IMPORTANT ELEMENT IN DESIGN AND ITS APPROPRIATENESS SHOULD ALWAYS BE ASSESSED. ONE SHOULD ALWAYS ASK WHETHER OR NOT THIS FENCE OR THIS PATIO OR THIS WALKWAY OR, AS HERE, THIS WALL, CAN BE MADE BETTER THROUGH ORNAMENTATION. HERE, IN A TIGHT SPACE CLOSELY BORDERED BY TALL BUILDINGS, THE TILES DRAW IN LIGHT AND BRIGHTNESS. THEY HELP REMOVE THE WALL FROM THE REALM OF THE FUNCTIONAL AND ELEVATE IT CLOSER TO THE REALM OF ART. ITS SURFACE IS PART OF THE DESIGN MOTIF AND CONTRIBUTES TO THE SENSE OF CHEERFUL GRACE.

It is often desirable and effective, in small urban gardens, to bring the garden up to the entry point so that stepping out of the dwelling envelops one in the garden. In the preceding project (page 112), a path beckoning onward to possibilities just glimpsed generated this effect, supported by a planted container set beside the door. Here, the raised bed against the door wall on the left and the raised brick planter against the building on the right achieve this end. A step out the door is a step into the garden.

An additional planter, placed just in front of the garden entrance, enhances the effect of envelopment. It partially screens the patio area from view while delineating two pathways, inviting the visitor further into the garden, offering alternative routes, and contributing to the garden's intrigue and surprise. No matter how often one enters this garden, one must always discover it anew. One must enter the garden and proceed until it is fully revealed; this gives it a slight touch of magic and expansion.

As we saw in the project on page 112, paying a few feet of surface area to buy another dimension of mystery is space well spent. Here, one low, curvy planter is home to bamboo, which with its leafy abundance makes the perfect enclosure to the patio area. Its foliage creates interesting patterns and shadows, and it screens the view toward the building without confining.

Though taking a bit of primary living space, this low planter serves two important compensatory functions: It adds a touch of discovery and surprise and screens the building from the patio.

Rectangular paving would not have worked in this garden. In the first project (page 12), curving brick walls were effectively combined with rectangular paving, but with river stones worked in to keep it from being too regulated. Here, odd-shaped and -sized pieces of stone have the same influence, contributing to the relaxed, carefree feeling this garden was intended to convey.

Try a Liquid Focal Point

The water garden is a vital element of this design. It anchors the entire space, which otherwise would have no focal point, and it captures the spirit of the garden. Built on a curve and inlaid with tiles, it harmonizes with the whole while invigorating it with the motion and sound of cascading water. It brings life to the garden within another dimension and holds the garden in its reflection. Though the garden would be a pleasant place without the water feature, with it, Mediterranean haven is born. The little pool is a symbol of the garden as a whole.

Though the haven is tiny, one quickly realizes in it that a garden is not a single place. As one moves through it, every change of position offers new views and experiences—some subtle, some dramatic. The garden seen through the bamboo—and it often is seen through the bamboo—is not the same place seen from beside the water feature. The paving, the walls, the vines growing on the lattice, the bower of cherry leaves and blossoms above, the ferns and other foliage and flowering plants offer a constantly changing array of vignettes—all within a private place, unified by theme and designed to satisfy its owners.

Curves and Spaces

ONE OF THE CHIEF VALUES OF CURVED WALLS AND BORDERS IS THAT AS LONG AS THEY CURVE OUT JUST ENOUGH TO ALLOW ABUNDANT PLANTING, THEY CAN ALSO BE MADE QUITE NARROW ON THE IN-CURVES. THIS CREATES A SENSE OF EXPANSION AS WELL AS REAL, USABLE SPACE FOR OUTDOOR LIVING.

The heart of the garden.

Randomly shaped and sized flagging contributes to the relaxed, flowing quality of the garden.

Though small, this garden offers many views.

Lessons from a Small Garden

Design theme
The contrast between the characteristics of the site and the qualities of the owners was so glaring that the design feeling arose readily as a need to bring the two into harmony. It was then just a matter of fleshing out the design with particulars.

Organization of space
One primary living area surrounded by planting, with a graceful access and egress created by an isolated planter. This planter creates a flow through the garden while screening the building from the primary area.

Structure
The low walls, the water garden, and the isolated, low planter.

Boundary structure
Wood fence topped with lattice, which generates privacy without being claustrophobic.

5. Combination of materials
Brick, lightened and made more cheerful with colored tiles, random stone, wood, and plants all combine to create an informal, friendly setting.

Proportion
The small space required narrow beds and, therefore, low walls. Paved and planted areas are about equal.

Summary of Details
The colored tiles, the undulation of the walls, the water garden, and the plant combinations.

Rustic Surprise

Creating the Illusion of Space

Complexity Level 3

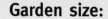

Once the existing perennials were put to the side, the open aspect of the original site became starkly apparent.

Garden size:
17 feet wide × 40 feet deep
(5.2 meters wide × 12.2 meters deep)

As the before image (on page 124, bottom) shows, this open scene of pretty plants was nevertheless devoid of interest. Not only was the whole space instantly and completely apparent, the plants offered little variation in size and shape. The garden was two-dimensional and conveyed neither visual nor experiential pleasure. The owner, who is an avid gardener and one-time farm owner, wanted the landscape to project an earthy, organic quality that was at once simple, playful, and interesting.

The after images show the garden the first year after construction, before planting was completed. Even at this stage, the difference is considerable. Not only does the space seem larger and more interesting, it is also more inviting and seems to offer much more in the way of experiential possibilities. What created this?

The garden after transformation, before the last stage of planting was completed.

Small Garden ——●—— Wisdom	**Generate the illusion of greater space in a small garden by holding back some of the view:**
	✳ Make paths meander rather than go straight to the living areas.
	✳ Screen separate living areas with trees and other plantings.
	✳ Hide boundaries: out of sight, out of mind.

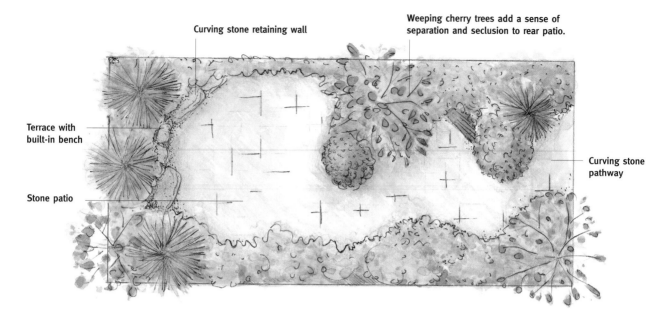

Curving stone retaining wall

Weeping cherry trees add a sense of separation and seclusion to rear patio.

Terrace with built-in bench

Stone patio

Curving stone pathway

Curved Paths Belong in Informal Gardens

IN AN INFORMAL GARDEN, CURVING PATHS ARE NOT ONLY APPROPRIATE, THEY ARE EFFECTIVE. IN FORMAL GARDENS, STRAIGHT PATHS ARE BASIC TO THE OVERALL SCHEME AND AESTHETIC; THEY ARE REQUIRED BY THE LAWS OF SYMMETRY AND CONTRIBUTE TO THE INTENDED EFFECT. BUT GARDENS CHARACTERIZED BY NATURAL FORMS, CURVING LINES HARMONIZE AND MAXIMIZE. HAD THE PATH IN THIS GARDEN BEEN MADE STRAIGHT, THE VIEW TO THE TERMINUS OF THE GARDEN WOULD HAVE BEEN UNOBSTRUCTED, AND ALL SENSE OF DISCOVERY AND SURPRISE WOULD HAVE BEEN OBLITERATED. WITH A CURVE, ROUNDING THE BEND IS PREREQUISITE TO DISCOVERING WHAT IS BEYOND.

As the before image shows, this open scene of pretty plants was nevertheless devoid of interest. Not only was the whole space instantly and completely apparent, the plants offered little variation in size and shape. The garden was two-dimensional and conveyed neither visual nor experiential pleasure. The owner, an avid gardener and one-time farm owner, wanted the landscape to project an earthy, organic quality that was at once simple, playful, and interesting.

The after images show the garden the first year after construction, before planting was completed. Even at this stage, the difference is considerable. Not only does the space seem larger and more interesting, it is also more inviting and seems to offer much more in the way of experiential possibilities. What created this?

This two-dimensional canvas of pretty plants lacked dimensionality, interest, and surprise.

Hold Back Some of the View

Ample space in the foreground, with a reasonably wide path leading to a partially visible space to the rear of a property, implies greater dimensionality. How so? Having one area leading to another that leads to yet another makes the space seem as if it cannot be very small, and when the boundaries of half-hidden portions of the garden are unknown, then it gives the illusion that they do not exist at all.

The meandering path is both a natural element and possible because the main outdoor living area was placed in the rear of this informally styled garden. This configuration allows the entire garden to be an event, an experience, rather than simply a visual phenomenon—so often the case when the living area is restricted to the front of the garden, from which one only views its remainder.

Of course, the path did not need to meander, but making it do so amplifies the experience of moving through the garden. Equally as important, the view to the rear is partially blocked from all locations in the front. In these images, the plants have not yet grown in, but within a few years, the weeping cherry trees staggered on both sides of the walk will make an effective screen from front to back, adding to the mystery of the garden as well as to the privacy of the rear patio area. As the plants mature, the degree of separation and seclusion will be enhanced.

Left: Structural, spatial, and textural alterations transform the site into an inviting garden.

Above: View from the front area toward the rear patio.

Employ Walls for Multiple Purposes

This bench, built as part of the retaining wall, adds visual interest and, with a few cushions, is a comfortable place to rest.

The rear section of the garden featured a raised, straight terrace, several feet deep and high, sloping down to grade. Here, a free-form patio was built, large enough to accommodate small parties. In keeping with the natural, informal style of this garden, at the base of the embankment a footing was carved out in an S-curve and a dry-laid wall built to retain the soil.

Apart from the practical purpose of retaining the soil, the wall provides several other services. Being several feet high and built of stone, it gives a sense of structure and containment to this end of the garden. It has a built-in bench that offers visual appeal and, with a few cushions thrown down, a comfortable place to lounge without the clutter of chairs.

Finally, consider the construction of the wall, which is built, not stacked. Had only a flat stone (in this case the reddish Pennsylvania or Amish stone) been used, it would have been stacked with one stone simply laid next to another, course upon course. Although appealing, it would not have been nearly as interesting or appropriate. Instead, a variety of stone types with many shapes was employed, making a built wall necessary. In this type of construction, the wall is not laid in even courses but is built around the odd-shaped stones. This gives the wall flow and motion—an organic quality—that harmonizes with the garden scheme as a whole, helping, however subliminally perceived, bring unity to the garden. The final effect is an informal, organic garden unified through repetition of form and line. It both invites exploration and satisfies the impulse to do so.

Above and Opposite: The organically built dry wall adds visual interest and carries the theme of rustic surprise.

Take a Garden to Its Limit, Literally

ONE OF THE BEST WAYS TO MAXIMIZE USE AND ENJOYMENT OF A GARDEN IS TO PLACE THE MAIN OUTDOOR LIVING AREA, OR THE MOST INTERESTING AND VISUALLY ATTRACTIVE AREA, IN THE MOST REMOTE CORNER. IN THE FIRST INSTANCE, THE GARDEN BECOMES A PLACE THROUGH WHICH ONE TRAVELS IN ORDER TO ARRIVE AT THE DESIRED DESTINATION. NOTHING IS MORE EFFECTIVE THAN THIS IN ADDING THE DIMENSION OF PERSONAL EXPERIENCE TO THAT OF VISUAL APPEAL. THE RESULT: A SPACE THAT IS NOT ONLY SATISFYING TO BEHOLD BUT A PLEASURE TO BE IN AND MOVE THROUGH.

WHEN A GARDEN IS MEANT TO BE VIEWED FROM SOME VANTAGE POINT, SUCH AS A DECK WHERE MOST OF THE OUTDOOR LIVING IS DONE, SCATTERING ELEMENTS OF INTEREST THROUGHOUT AND PLACING A SIGNIFICANT COMPONENT TO THE VERY REAR OF THE GARDEN MAXIMIZES ITS POTENTIAL. TOO OFTEN, THE REAR PORTION IS LEFT AS A MERE MASS OF FOLIAGE, UNSEEN AND UNAPPRECIATED, WHEREAS A PIECE OF SCULPTURE, FOR EXAMPLE, WOULD ATTRACT THE EYE AND GIVE THE VIEWER GREATER ENJOYMENTS.

Lessons from a Small Garden

Design theme
Organic informality, based on the excellent soil, ideal for cultivation, and the history of the client.

Organization of space
A front area large enough for functional elements (storage shed, compost bin), from which a meandering path leads to a rear area with a free-form patio and dry-laid retaining wall. All else is planting beds.

Structure
The stone walkway edged in stone and patio and the rear dry wall.

Boundary structure
One side is open to the adjacent property; the other sides are bounded by wood fences.

Combination of materials
Stones and plants.

Proportion
Half planted areas, half unplanted, with the rear patio roughly balanced with the walk and front areas combined. The path is about 3 feet (.9 m) wide, which is ample without feeling confining and without taking too much planting space.

Summary of Details
The stonework, the lattice planted in an espaliered apple, and other plantings yet to come into their own.

A Wild, Romantic Tangle

Building an Ancient Ruins

**Complexity
Level 4**

Garden size:
17 feet wide × 28 feet deep
(5.2 meters wide × 8.5 meters deep)

As the before image shows, the qualities of mystery and surprise were notably lacking in this site. The entire space was flat, completely apparent, instantly apprehended, and all too visible from surrounding properties. Here, however, an entirely different approach from the previous examples was used to create an air of mystery and infuse the element of surprise.

*Above: The garden before
transformation.*

Flowing water and well-placed stone combine with a controlled disorder of planting to create enchantment and romance in this small city garden.

Small Garden — Wisdom	**To transport garden visitors to another place and time, follow this plan:**
	❁ Articulate a concrete theme. ❁ Ensure that every rock and leaf expresses the stated theme. ❁ Employ unusual materials, both in structures and in plantings.

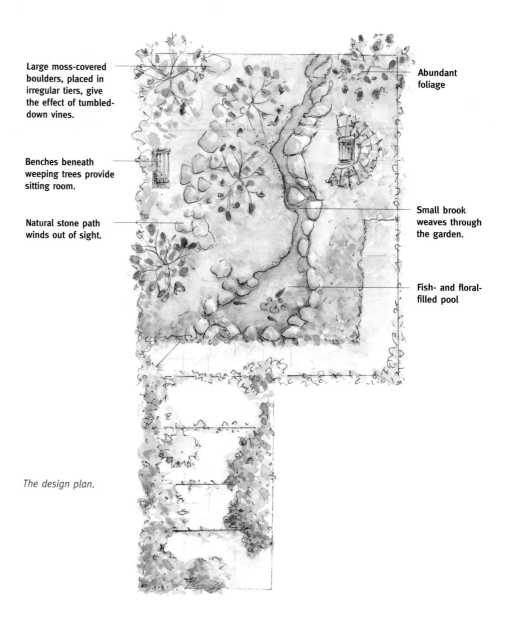

Large moss-covered boulders, placed in irregular tiers, give the effect of tumbled-down vines.

Benches beneath weeping trees provide sitting room.

Natural stone path winds out of sight.

Abundant foliage

Small brook weaves through the garden.

Fish- and floral-filled pool

The design plan.

The homeowners specified that they wanted a wild, romantic tangle, but what exactly that meant and how it was to be achieved were open questions. Certainly, such a theme invites numerous interpretations. As is so often the case, however, existing elements—which, in conjunction with the owners' tastes—in this case a predilection for classical antiquity—suggested the direction of the garden's development.

There were a few old stones lying around, including a piece of quarried granite (now visible in the upper left of the garden). Among these finds lurked the genius of the place—the notion of an ancient ruins on a once lovely site, cloaked behind a luxuriance of plantings—and became the theme around which the garden would be created.

Ideas came quickly: remnants of some old structure wildly overgrown with vines and other plants of a pagan feel, an artesian well spilling into a small brook weaving through the garden and terminating in a small fish- and flora-filled pool. A small, natural path would invite the visitor to explore, winding out of sight to the rear of the garden. A small, paved area, now becoming a sculpture court, would provide access and a vantage point from which to enjoy the garden. To meet the requirement of being visually appealing from the windows above, the garden would be bold and dramatic.

In short, this garden would become a wild, romantic ruin with an ancient, classical feel, endowed with private bowers, flowing water, and a plethora of plant species. But as charming as this sounds, how does it create mystery and surprise? Except for where the path winds out of sight in the upper left, all areas of the garden are visible, yet the overwhelming response this garden evokes in every visitor is one of astonishment—and no matter how long one sits within the garden, an aura of mystery remains. Why is this? Part of the answer lies in the theme of the garden itself. The last thing anyone expects to find in an urban backyard is an ancient ruin complete with artesian well, babbling brook, and beautiful fish.

Evoke an Exotic World with Exotic Materials

Another and important element of this garden's impact as a place both mysterious and surprising is the materials selected and the manner of their use. Tons of moss rock prominently displayed, pieces of weathered capitals and other architectural elements strewn romantically about, sculpture and running water, purposefully placed, a wealth of plant species interwoven to create dramatic contrasts and pleasing harmonies—each contributes to the sense of wildness and all combine to create a world that seems to belong to another time and place, one slightly pagan, natural, vital, and richly mysterious.

The manner in which the materials were used, in this garden more than in any other of these projects, perhaps, is particularly significant. Quality of construction is always important, but when creating natural elements such as streams and pools, quality considerations go beyond values of good craftsmanship. The aura of mystery attempted here, and the quality of surprise and discovery it elicits, would not exist if not for the care taken in working with the various materials—the placement of stone, the layering of dimensions through the creation of tiers, and the depth and nature of the planting. Certainly this added to the cost of the project, but without this level of attention, the resultant garden would have failed in its expression.

From a desolate site to a wild, romantic tangle.

Beauty is Always Interesting— Interesting Is Not Always Beautiful

EVERYONE BECOMES TIRED OF THE USUAL. THE TENDENCY, ESPECIALLY AMONG DESIGNERS AND ARTISTS, IS TO DO SOMETHING DIFFERENT WITHIN THEIR MEDIUM SIMPLY BECAUSE IT IS DIFFERENT. ALTHOUGH THIS APPROACH CAN LEAD TO INTERESTING RESULTS, IT DOES OFTEN NOT LEAD TO BEAUTIFUL ONES. IN GARDENS, REALLY GOOD DESIGN IS UNUSUAL ENOUGH THAT THERE IS NO NEED TO BE OVERLY INVENTIVE IN ORDER TO CREATE A PLACE OF BEAUTY AND INTEREST. THE ARTIST MUST, AT TIMES, RESIST THE IMPULSE TO DO SOMETHING DIFFERENT AND DRAMATIC, JUST TO MAKE HIS CREATION INTERESTING.

Fish enjoy the cascading water and swim the length of the stream.

Call on Dramatic Means to Express Dramatic Themes

When creating a garden based on an articulated theme, every component must contribute to expressing it. When working with natural elements such as streams and pools, every detail of construction either adds to or detracts from the final effect.

In this project, multiple dimensions and planes were essential, as was the natural look of the source well, the stream, and pool. The before image shows a flat, static site, one without change, motion, and drama. To alleviate this, several hundred cubic feet of soil were used to raise the rear and sides of the property. These elevations were then sculpted into nooks and channels, adding to the drama by giving them an irregular horizontal line as well as a cascading vertical aspect.

Large stones were used to create irregular tiers, giving the effect of a tumbled-down ruin.

A particularly primitive-looking natural stone called moss rock was used to retain these elevations—again, in irregular fashion—but placed in such a way as to suggest a previous structure—the bones of a ruin. As the in-progress images show, the site was dramatically transformed even at this stage.

A machine for manipulating the largest stones had to be invented and built in order to place the 1500-pound stones such that the artesian well would have a natural appearance. Considerable care was employed in the placement of the smaller rocks and stones as well.

Meaning in Materials

MATERIALS CAN HAVE A PROFOUND EFFECT ON THE EMOTIONAL RESPONSE TO A GARDEN. LARGE, MOSS-COVERED BOULDERS, FOR EXAMPLE, ARE DRAMATIC, NATURALLY IMPRESSIVE, AND, WEIGHING IN AT 1 1/2 TONS, SOMETIMES FRIGHTENING. WHEN WELL PLACED IN A BEAUTIFUL GARDEN, ESPECIALLY IN CONJUNCTION WITH WATER AND PLANTS, THEY ARE SATISFYING AND ADD AN ELEMENT OF EXCITEMENT AND INTRIGUE. WATER, ESPECIALLY WATER IN MOTION, ALWAYS EXCITES AND ENLIVENS. PLANTS, INDIVIDUALLY AND IN COMBINATION, CAN HAVE A DRAMATIC AS WELL AS SUBTLE EMOTIONAL IMPACT ON THE BEHOLDER.

Above left: This machine, designed by the author and built by a shipbuilder, lifted and deftly placed the 1500-pound stones.

Above middle and right: Precise placement of the stones gave the source well a natural appearance.

Seek Plants Outside the Range of the Familiar

The final element that helps this garden succeed as a mysterious, if not mystical, paradise is the plants employed and their placement. Familiar plants of a tame nature were explicitly avoided. Instead, cryptomeria, ferns, grasses, barberry, leocothoe, red-twig dogwood, and oak-leaf hydrangea were planted.

The clipped boxwood, often used in formal gardens, is left unclipped to form a wonderful, rich, wild element and to provide the sweet perfume of their otherwise inconspicuous blossoms—a romantic addition. They also make a fine evergreen backdrop to other plants, and the lovely light green of the new growth is the quintessence of springtime.

Honeysuckle, fragrant rhododendron, climbing roses, sweet woodruff, violets, and other perennials also add fragrance, while the rampant growth of wisteria and the bold leaf of the oak-leaf hydrangea, aralia, and viburnum contribute to the pagan quality. Sitting in this garden beneath the canopy of flowering trees, surrounded by ruins, listening to the stream roil over rocks, and watching the fish swim its length, it is impossible not feel as if you have entered an old and magical world, always mysterious and forever surprising.

A rich tapestry of wild and woodsy-looking plants contribute to the mystery of this garden.

Design theme

Wild, romantic ruins ensconced in a tangle of rampant growth, suggested by the client's tastes and the existing stones and bones of the place. *(top left)*

Organization of space

The long axis is emphasized by the roughly parallel path and stream and by the planting that borders them both. About midway, spaces on both sides open where benches sit beneath weeping trees. *(top left)*

Structure

Boulders, used for the artesian well and to retain the irregular terraces; smaller rocks that define the stream and pool and balance with the abundant foliage.
(top and bottom right)

Boundary structure

Though fences now provide the boundary structure, these will, in time, be more appropriately covered with foliage and flowers.
(bottom left)

Combination of materials

Stone, plants, and water.

Proportion

Not a great consideration here. A wild quality was sought, so planting is much more profuse than usual. The main concern within the motif was to provide ample walking and adequate sitting room within the garden proper. *(top left)*

Summary of Details

Sculpture, randomly placed, appropriateness of stone placement in the stream, plant combinations, the spillways and falls in the stream, and small plants in niches between stones.

Lessons from a Small Garden

Directory of Materials

Garden Ornaments

Garden mosaic: A surface decoration made by inlaying various shaped, sized, and colored pieces of any variety of materials to form a picture or a pattern, often of a garden-related or romantic theme. Usually seen on a vertical surface, a mosaic can also adorn flat areas, particularly in small spaces, and can add considerably to the interest and enjoyment of a small space. *(see page 22)*

Garden tiles: Glazed or unglazed ceramic tiles that in colder regions need to be certified to be frostproof. They can be handmade, one-of-a-kind, or mass produced. *(see pages 12, 74, 116)*

Planters: Most commonly built of cedar, redwood, or pressure-treated wood and rectangular in shape, or of glazed or unglazed, fired clay, in which case they are often bowl shaped. Some gardens, such as rooftop gardens, can only be of planters, in which case a diversity of them often works best. Many gardens with ample planting space also benefit from the presence of planters as they provide a harmonizing architectural element within the garden. *(see pages 22, 54, 94, 98, 112)*

Statuary: Effective in both the formal and informal garden, particularly as a harmonizing balance to abundant foliage. *(see pages 22, 36, 128)*

Garden Plans

Elevation drawing: A schematic drawing showing some feature or area from a side view. Often used to show construction details.

Plan view drawing: A scaled drawing in which the property layout is viewed from above. This is the standard view for both architectural drawings and landscape drawings.

Rendering: An artistic drawing or painting showing a realistic representation of a proposed landscape. *(see all projects)*

Scaled drawing: A schematic layout of a property in which a specific measure on paper accurately represents a designated distance on the property. For landscape drawings, one-eighth scale is common, wherein 1 inch (3 cm) on the paper represents 8 feet (2.4 m) of real property distance.

Garden Structures

Arbor: Freestanding, generally arch-shaped structure, designed to create or accentuate an entry point between two areas. *(see pages 12, 22, 54, 68)*

Garden bench: In addition to providing seating, garden benches can add an element of warmth and welcome to a garden. *(see pages 44, 54, 76, 122, 128)*

Garden bench, built-in: A space-effective method of creating seating areas in small gardens; built as part of some primary structure, such as into a wall. *(see pages 12, 76, 122)*

Lattice: Panels of slats laid perpendicularly to one another either in a diagonal or square pattern. Generally made of either pressure-treated wood, cedar, redwood, or synthetic materials in order to withstand outdoor elements. Both the dimensions of the slats themselves and the spaces between them can vary considerably. Often used as an overlay to a solid fence. *(see pages 12, 62)*

Pergola: An arbor with a built-in bench, usually placed at a termination point within a garden, such as at the end of a garden walk. (*see page 98*)

Raised beds: Planting areas raised above the primary grade and usually stabilized by retaining walls. When built on level ground, it is usually necessary to place some barrier on the back side either to protect a fence or other existing structure from decay due to contact with soil or to retain the soil on that side. (*see pages 12, 22, 44, 54, 76, 116, 122*)

Retaining wall: Walls of any material used to retain the soil of a higher elevation. It is often important in the creation of such walls to include weep holes near the base to allow for drainage and to prevent the build up of water pressure that can, in time, push the wall over. (*see pages 12, 22, 44, 54, 76, 116, 122*)

Terracing: The creation of level, raised beds by cutting into an existing slope and lowering the high side while raising the low side. (*see pages 12, 22, 44, 54, 116, 122*)

Garden Styles

English garden: Characterized by a seemingly chaotic plethora of plants that is, in fact, quite specifically laid out with consideration of plant size, bloom time, and flower color. They often contain small walls of stone and brick and have about them a cottage charm. (*see page 22*)

Formal: A symmetrically laid out garden often endowed with a quality of sophisticated elegance conveyed through the use of classical forms and structures.

Mediterranean: Refers to the Spanish Mediterranean style of architecture. Gardens of this type are usually walled gardens ornamented with tiles and contain plants in pots and a fountain. (*see page 116*)

Organic: A style characterized by natural materials and curvy, not straight lines. (*see page 44*)

Romantic: A style intended to evoke romantic emotions through the use of scent, pleasing harmonies, beautiful color, and evocative structures such as arbors, pergolas, or water gardens. *(see pages 54, 128)*

Rustic: Ample use of natural, unfinished materials such as rough wood, natural stone, and large boulders in a casual arrangement contribute to the Rustic style. *(see page 122)*

Victorian: Natural materials combined in formal or semiformal arrangements, often with an abundance of ornament and powerful color combinations typify the Victorian garden. *(see page 54)*

Paving and Walls

Bluestone: A type of flagstone widely available in the northeastern United States, ranging in color from browns and greens to blue, blue-gray and gray. *(see pages 12, 44, 54, 62, 68, 76, 104, 128)*

Brick: Baked clay, usually cube-shaped and available in a variety of sizes and colors. One of the most ancient and versatile building materials, both inexpensive and easy to work with. In-ground constructions in temperate regions often used without mortar. In colder regions and for vertical constructions usually used with mortar. Combines well with many materials. *(see pages 12, 22, 94)*

Built wall: A wall of any kind of odd-shaped and odd-sized stone, built by working with the individual shapes of the stone, thereby requiring more skill in placement than is necessary in a laid-up wall. Can be with or without mortar. *(see pages 44, 54, 122)*

Concrete: A mixture of sand, gravel, and Portland cement, mixed with water to harden into a dense, strong, and solid mass. *(see pages 12, 76, 116)*

Concrete block: Preformed rectangular concrete units usually available in 4- or 8-inch (10 cm or 20 cm) thicknesses, 8 inches (20 cm) tall and 14, 16, or 18 inches (36 cm, 41 cm, or 46 cm) long. They can be solid or hollow core. *(see pages 12, 76)*

Coping/coping stones: The finished top or cap to a wall. This can be the same material as the wall, or a completely different material. *(see pages 12, 76)*

Dry-laid wall: A wall built without mortar. *(see pages 44, 54, 122)*

Fieldstone: A weathered, irregular-shaped stone often used without mortar in the creation of walls. *(see pages 22, 44, 54, 122)*

Flagstone: Any usually rectangular-(flag) shaped stone from less than an inch (3 cm) to several inches in thickness; used for paving. Generally available in a variety of sizes from 1 foot (30 cm) square to 4 feet by 4 feet (1.2 m × 1.2 m) or larger. The type and color of stone available for flagstone will vary from region to region and from stoneyard to stoneyard. Can be laid on sand, stone dust, directly on soil in temperate climates, or on a concrete base with cement. *(see pages 12, 44, 54, 62, 68, 76, 94, 104, 116, 122)*

Footing: A concrete foundation usually from several inches to a foot (8 cm to 20 cm) in thickness, the bottom of which is generally poured below the frost line. Used to support foundations. *(see pages 12, 76, 116)*

Foundation: A concrete or concrete-block structure built upon a footing and used to support walls and other structures. *(see pages 12, 76, 116)*

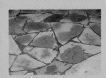

Irregular flagstone: Odd-shaped and odd-sized flagstone. *(see page 116)*

Laid-up wall:
A wall built by stacking stone on top of stone without mortar. So long as the joints in the course below are spanned by the stone above, this can both look good and be strong but is not generally meant as a load-bearing wall. *(see pages 22, 44, 54, 122)*

Manufactured wall block: An interlocking, manufactured concrete product used for easy construction of retaining walls. *(see page 36)*

Mortar: A cementitious material consisting primarily of Portland cement and lime. Combined with sand as an aggregate, it is used to bind masonry materials such as brick and stone into solid structures. *(see pages 12, 76, 94, 104, 116)*

Moss rock: A dense, natural stone available in a variety of sizes from about 50 pounds to several thousand pounds, often delivered with moss growing on it. Useful for rustic walls, along streams and adjacent to water falls. *(see page 128)*

River boulders: Similar to river rounds but larger. *(see pages 76, 128)*

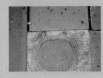

River flats: A smooth, ovular, relatively thin stone from several inches to a foot (8 cm to 30 cm) or more across; taken from river beds. Though naturally occurring where there are rivers, this stone is not carried by every stone yard. *(see pages 12, 76, 128)*

River pebbles: Smooth, usually oval-shaped stone, ranging in size from less than 1 inch (3 cm) across to several inches (8 cm) and in color from white through yellows, grays to black. *(see page 62)*

River rounds: Similar to river flats but less flat, more spherical. If used as a wall stone, they must be cemented.   *(see pages 62, 76, 128)*

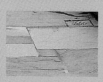

Slate: A paving stone much like bluestone but thinner, with a shinier surface. *(see page 94)*

Water Features

Formal pool: A symmetrical, in-ground or above-ground pool. *(see pages 54, 116)*

Natural pond: An in-ground pool made to look as if it is naturally occurring, not man-made. A pump recirculates the water through a hose and generally over a waterfall, back into the pool. The chief difficulty of construction is in making it look natural. *(see pages 44, 62, 128)*

Raised informal pool: A free-form, above-ground pool, usually asymmetrical in shape, as opposed to a formal pool, containing a pump that recirculates the water. *(see pages 12, 76)*

Stream: Usually originates from a waterfall or small pool, flowing into a larger pool. The two primary difficulties of construction are to make it look natural and to have the water flowing over, not under, the stones in the stream bed. *(see pages 76, 128)*

Waterfall: Most natural pools and streams will have a waterfall as the source. The usual mistake is to use stones that have never had water flowing over them and consequently don't look right in a waterfall. *(see pages 62, 76, 128)*

Wall fountain: An ornamental, self-contained unit consisting of a decorative source such as a lion's head from which water flows into an ornamental basin containing a pump. *(see pages 12, 68)*

About the Author

Keith Davitt has been designing, building, photographing, and writing about gardens across America and abroad for twenty years. His gardens and articles have appeared in numerous magazines including Fine Gardening, Country Gardens, Gardening How-To, Sunset, Horticulture, Period Homes, Traditional Building, Passage Actualité, and others. He recently won the Herald Award for Excellence in Garden Communication in which several of his gardens were featured. For the last decade he has worked in the New York City area in the creation of private and public gardens where he has developed techniques for enlarging small garden spaces through design. The author can be contacted through his Web site at www.gardenviews.com.

Acknowledgments

Foremost, let me extend my gratitude to my clients, without whose trust and belief none of this would have been possible. To make a garden for someone is both a privilege and a responsibility, and I hope that I merited that privilege and lived up to that responsibility.

I thank my New York crew, Juan, Enriche, and Roliejo Juarez, who treated each project as if it were their own. They strove in good cheer to do everything well and, when the going got tough, as it not infrequently did, they pressed through with me to find lasting solutions to difficult problems.

My thanks to Steven Potenzano for his superb irrigation systems that keep these gardens growing.

My especial thanks to Ludmila and Jacqueline McKannay for their beautiful, hand-carved tiles that now adorn two of my gardens.

Thanks to Ann Fox, my ever helpful project manager in the creation of this book, to Martha Wetherill whose wonderful strength, knowledge, experience, and diplomacy pulled us over some difficult hills, and to Rockport Publishers and their consistent, cohesive approach to getting the job done.

And last, yet first and always, my thanks to thee, Jacqueline, for reasons too numerous to name.